D0281272

# Understanding advocacy for children and young people

Sheffield Hallam University
Learning and Information Services

Withdrawn From Stock

# Understanding advocacy for children and young people

*Jane Boylan and Jane Dalrymple*

Open University Press

Open University Press
McGraw-Hill Education
McGraw-Hill House
Shoppenhangers Road
Maidenhead
Berkshire
England
SL6 2QL

email: enquiries@openup.co.uk
world wide web: www.openup.co.uk

and Two Penn Plaza, New York, NY 10121-2289, USA

First published 2009

Copyright © Boylan and Dalrymple 2009

All rights reserved. Except for the quotation of short passages for the purposes of
criticism and review, no part of this publication may be reproduced, stored in a
retrieval system, or transmitted, in any form or by any means, electronic,
mechanical, photocopying, recording or otherwise, without the prior written
permission of the publisher or a licence from the Copyright Licensing Agency
Limited. Details of such licences (for reprographic reproduction) may be obtained
from the Copyright Licensing Agency Ltd of Saffron House, 6–10 Kirby Street,
London, EC1N 8TS.

A catalogue record of this book is available from the British Library

ISBN-13: 978-0-33-522373-2 (pb) 978-0-33-522372-5 (hb)
ISBN-10: 0335223737 (pb) 0335223729 (hb)

Library of Congress Cataloging-in-Publication Data
CIP data applied for

Typeset by RefineCatch Limited, Bungay, Suffolk
Printed in the UK by Bell and Bain Ltd, Glasgow.

Fictitious names of companies, products, people, characters and/or data that may
be used herein (in case studies or in examples) are not intended to represent any
real individual, company, product or event.

**Mixed Sources**
Product group from well-managed
forests and other controlled sources
www.fsc.org   Cert no. TT-COC-002769
© 1996 Forest Stewardship Council
FSC

The **McGraw·Hill** Companies

# Contents

For Ian and Paul

# Acknowledgements

We have been fortunate while writing this book in having the support of colleagues, friends, our families and our respective universities, who have provided us with the space and encouragement to complete the work. Special thanks are due to all those who have commented on draft chapters and engaged with the issues, offering thoughtful advice and observations. Particular thanks go to the Children's Legal Centre, Graham Allan, Roger Bishop, Alison Brammer, Suzy Braye, Beverley Burke, Mekada Graham, Kate Mercer, Harry Shier, Barry Percy-Smith, Andy Pithouse, Bob Pitt, Jane Tarr, Neil Thompson, Jackie Murphy, Peter Jenkins and Charlotte Williams. We are also grateful to Jack Fray at Open University Press for his patience and support. We owe a special debt to John Pierson, who kindly read the complete draft manuscript and offered stimulating comments. Finally, the book could not have been completed without the support of Ian and Paul and the tolerance of Richard, Tim, Ciara and Pam.

The authors and publisher would like to thank the following for permission to reproduce copyright material in the form of extracts, figures and tables:

Sounds Good Project (2005) *Growing Up Speaking Out*. Reprinted by permission of the Advocacy Resource Exchange (ARX) – Box 5.6.

Scottish Executive (2001) Ten Dos and Don'ts for Commissioning Advocacy. Reprinted by permission of the Scottish Government Health Directives – Box 7.6.

Cardiff University School of Social Sciences/Social Inclusion Research Unit, University of North East Wales/ Department of Child Health, Wales College of Medicine for use of material previously published in Pithouse et al. (2005) *A Study of Advocacy Services for Children and Young People in Wales: A Key Messages Report*.

Jessica Kingsley Publishers for use of material previously published in Oliver and Dalrymple (2008) *Developing Advocacy for Children and Young People*.

# Foreword

During the debate on what became the Children Act 2004, I reflected that if 'Every Child Matters' should fail it would be for want of a wholesale commitment to children's rights and the effective advocacy to make them real.

While there continues to be further progress as part of what I still believe will come to be the great transformation of children's services and children's lives at the turn of the twenty-first century, there is still a very long way to go. The recent debate on the Children and Young People's Bill surely demonstrates that the government is still far too wary of unleashing the energy and insight of young people even though this would provoke and sustain the very cultural change that Every Child Matters requires.

On the other hand, there are limits to legislation and its accompanying policy and guidance. However hopeful the overall situation, there will always be dangers from adults and adult-dominated systems setting the framework within which the vitality and urgency of young people can be contained. Whatever our role – and social worker, politician and grandparent are three of mine – it is vital that our view of young people and their views is constantly refreshed by our direct contact with them and their own lives as they develop and grow.

Jane Boylan and Jane Dalrymple have given us a textbook for our times. This is a major review of the constantly developing context of children's rights, a wise guide to the full range of issues and a principled reminder that children and young people know a lot more about their lives than we do.

Anyone who purports to work with or care about children and young people should read it and use it now.

Hilton Dawson

# Introduction

She was watching a child build a sandcastle and not succeeding and found herself very surprised the child did not lose his temper; she decided to help the child. Much later, still thinking about the child's self control, she suddenly realised that the child wasn't building a sandcastle at all – but that she, the adult, assumed that was what he was doing and therefore that he was failing. If we look at children from the height of the little hill we have captured, they are bound to seem unsuccessful adults. Unfortunately we have the power to act on our own arrogant and mistaken assessment of the situation, and generally do so. So we hurry on desperately trying to organise the chaos that is building up in our own untranquil mind, listening only to what the child would mean if he were the adult and not what the child is saying.

(Leila Berg, cited in Harvey 1993: 159)

The starting point for us in writing this book has been the challenge to embrace a fundamental ideological shift in the way that we think about and respond to children and young people. Our desire to undertake this study began as a natural development of our respective interests and from a wish to contribute to knowledge and an understanding of the role of independent advocacy within children's and young people's services. The concept of independent advocacy with children and young people is relatively new. Despite the policy and legislative frameworks of the Children Acts 1989 and 2004, The Children (Scotland) Act 1995, the Children (Northern Ireland) Order 1995 and the United Nations Convention on the Rights of the Child 1989 (UNCRC), decision making for children and young people using health, education and social welfare services has been dominated by adult agendas and frames of reference that can silence the views of children and young people. Nevertheless, the political context of advocacy for children and young people has changed over the last twenty years and children's rights and advocacy services now operate across the four nations of the UK.

Although the changing political context of advocacy can only be welcomed, Rees's (1991) assertion that to achieve a desired outcome the advocacy task may be assisted by an understanding of power in different contexts is still pertinent. For him, an 'awareness of injustice should be coupled to a determination to pursue the interests of the parties who are subject to injustice, and to do so with a conviction uncluttered by consideration of tactics and compromise' (Rees 1991: 145). This indicates the radical potential of advocacy to promote the voice and agency of children and young people. A central activity for us therefore in writing this book has been to interrogate the contemporary context in which advocacy operates alongside our understanding of oppression and critical practice. From there we have examined the power relations that exist between adults and children and young people in various contexts to present a critical appraisal of the context of advocacy practice.

It is important at this point to look briefly at our use of the term 'advocate'. Most practitioners working with children and young people have, within their remit, an advocacy role. They use advocacy skills to promote the rights and interests of services users. There are also a wide range of voluntary, independent and private organizations providing various services for children and young people in particular situations, such as young asylum seekers, young homeless people, young offenders, young disabled people, and young gay and lesbian people. An essential part of the work of these agencies is advocacy, although the work that they do is unlikely to be identified specifically as advocacy and they do not promote themselves as an advocacy service. Most services that expressly locate themselves as advocacy services generally work with children and young people who are (1) living away from home in residential care, education establishments, secure accommodation or young offender institutions, (2) using identified services (e.g. mental health), (3) involved in formal decision-making processes such as child protection conferences or family group conferences, or (4) making a formal complaint in relation to health services, social services or education. It is notable here that advocacy services appear to mirror the groupings of children and young people within statutory services (Oliver et al. 2004; Pithouse et al. 2005).

Our aim in writing this book is to inform and generate discussion about advocacy practice in all these situations and also to reflect on the particular issues affecting independent advocates. We hope that in an area of practice that is relatively new it will contribute to a dialogue that will, in turn, work towards creating a culture of advocacy. This book therefore is aimed at independent advocates, those who use advocacy skills within their professional role, as well as policy makers and commissioners of advocacy services. We hope that it will be relevant for all practitioners who are passionate about promoting social justice for children and young people. We believe that this is essential if advocacy is to contribute to building a climate in which children and young people can determine the shape of independent advocacy services and challenge their construction by adult service providers. An element of our contribution to the dialogue is the integration of advocacy theory, policy and practice throughout. For that reason, this is not a book about advocacy skills. We begin by taking a historical overview of advocacy within professional practice. This sets the scene for understanding dilemmas and issues facing social workers and other professionals who have to balance their traditional advocacy role with the constraints of agency policies and limited resources. The role of independent advocates is examined, with consideration given to their place in the provision and delivery of services. Finally, we discuss the practice of advocacy and the challenges that advocacy poses in the delivery of children's and young people's services.

Creating knowledge about advocacy practice occurs within discourses of childhood, children's rights, voice and resistance, which we will consider in the early chapters of this book. In Chapter 1, we examine the historical context of advocacy for children and young people. We chart the development of advocacy by locating it within professional practice. The impact of the service user movement and the growth in literature pertaining to advocacy with children and young people has led to an increasing awareness that they should have access to an independent advocate as a potential mechanism for promoting their participatory rights. This chapter refers to policy and legislative mandates and how contemporary advocacy practice is shaped by both national and international initiatives.

In Chapter 2, we go on to consider how advocacy for children and young people has emerged through their disempowered status. The extent to which children and young people are allowed to participate in decision making is influenced by perceptions of childhood by adults with power to enforce them. The rationale for limiting children's rights has been ascribed to a desire to protect children's weakness, vulnerability and innocence. The context of independent advocacy will be examined through the impact of rights discourses on legislation and practice. Key policies and international instruments, such as the UNCRC, will be explored. Readers will be encouraged to consider what is meant by rights and different types of rights will be looked at as part of this discussion. Consideration of the construction of childhood and discourses of children's rights will facilitate analysis of the issues. An awareness of power is at the heart of debates about young people's rights, advocacy and participation. We therefore go on to consider the relationship between advocacy and participation in more detail in Chapter 3. From this, discussion about the discourse of voice leads to an examination of the extent to which advocacy is a potential force for resistance.

The first three chapters provide the context for discussing questions surrounding definitions of advocacy in Chapter 4. The contested nature of advocacy will be explored through analysis of theoretical perspectives, service user mandates and legislative imperatives. Debates about advocacy at both micro and macro levels will be considered in this chapter. Chapter 5 will then go on to look at established forms of advocacy. While various forms of advocacy co-exist, there are fundamental differences, despite the common goal of empowering service users and challenging oppressive systems. These will be outlined in this chapter. This then leads to an exploration in Chapter 6 of the nature and scope of models for providing advocacy, including case and systemic advocacy, passive and active ways of working, and service approaches. We also present our own model based on the participatory frameworks discussed in Chapter 3. In Chapter 7, we start to bring together the arguments traced through previous chapters to explore the extent to which advocacy may be a tool for anti-oppressive practice – to challenge constructions of children and childhood. The impact of the contradictory role of professionals, who have both an empowering and regulatory role, will also be examined. In the final chapter, we look at contemporary advocacy practice and its potential to enable children and young people to come to voice. We bring together the key messages and debates that have emerged through previous chapters in relation to theory, policy and practice to reflect on the reality of advocacy practice for young people, advocates and professional practitioners.

Independent advocacy is a dynamic and continuously developing way of working with children and young people. Its profile has changed significantly over the last twenty years and the fact that advocacy and participation rights for children and young people are now recognized in policy and legislation can only be a step in the right direction. We believe, however, that if advocacy for children and young people is to make a difference, advocates need to resist discourse determinism, where young people and their advocates are mechanically positioned in discourses without any room to explicate the possibilities for resistance and change. What is also difficult is the implicit dichotomy between the 'heroic' advocate and child care professionals who may appear to be positioned as negative, even abusive. It has been important for us not to position advocates either as crusaders (which can become part of the problem for children and young people) or as part of statutory service systems for children and young people. Rather, we have tried to contribute to a discourse of child and youth advocacy as a way of resisting the oppression of children and young people and enabling them to come to voice.

# 1 Charting the development of advocacy for children and young people

Children's development state makes them particularly vulnerable to human rights violations; their opinions are still rarely taken into account; most children have no vote and cannot play a meaningful role in the political process that determines governments' response to human rights; children encounter significant problems in using the judicial system to protect their rights or to seek remedies for violations of their rights; and children's access to organisations that may protect their rights is generally limited.

(Committee on the Rights of the Child 2003: Para. 5)

## Introduction

The origins of advocacy for children and young people can be located in the 'child-saving' era (Herbert and Mould 1992) of the nineteenth and early twentieth centuries, and understood in the context of the 'historical status' of 'welfare children' (Frost and Stein 1989: 132)[1]. When Eglantine Jebb founded Save the Children Fund in 1922, she campaigned for the protective rights of children. She also drafted the 1922 Declaration of Children's Rights, which was endorsed by the League of Nations in 1924. The child's need to be protected and cared for was central, coupled with moral concerns that 'the child must be brought up in the consciousness that its talents must be devoted to the service of its fellow men'. At this stage, however, there was a notable absence of political or participatory rights for children and young people. Progress was slow – subsequent declarations, including the 1959 Declaration on the Rights of the Child, continued to have a paternalistic theme and advocated protectionism with the inclusion of the concept of 'best interests' appearing for the first time.

In the 1970s, however, came recognition that children and young people have the right to a voice and to be heard. The International Year of the Child in 1979 raised the national profile of children's rights, serving as a catalyst for several developments that have influenced and informed the landscape of social welfare provision. Pressure groups and organizations advocating on behalf of children began to emerge. These included the Children's Legal Centre, the Scottish Law Centre, Justice for Children and the Child Poverty Action Group. At the same time, the Labour Party proposed a Minister for Children and a Children's Commissioner. Here again progress was slow, and it took a further twenty four years for a Children's Commissioner to be established in England[2], following vigorous lobbying by Children's Rights campaigners (Newell 1991, 2000 CRAE 2003). In other nations of the United Kingdom (UK), Children's Commissioners were established earlier with more powers than the Commissioner in England (see Box 1.4 later in this chapter).

The need for children and young people using health and social care services to have access to independent advocacy gained impetus following the implementation of the Children Act 1989 in England and Wales, the Children (Scotland) Act 1995 and the Children (Northern Ireland) Order 1995, and adoption of the United Nations Convention on the Rights of the Child (UNCRC). The UNCRC, which had been formally adopted by the UN General Assembly in 1989, was ratified by the UK in 1991. By ratifying the Convention the government was stating its intention to comply with it and to make regular reports to the UN Convention on the Rights of the Child about its implementation. To encourage implementation of the UNCRC, an independent project – the Children's Rights Development Unit – was set up for three years in 1992. Their systematic analysis of the extent to which law, policy and practice in the UK complied with the UNCRC identified the lack of any real attempt at implementation (Children's Rights Development Unit 1994). Nevertheless, since then the Convention has had an impact on the development of advocacy and informs National Standards for the Provision of Advocacy Services (Department of Health 2002; Welsh Assembly Government 2003).

Various forms of advocacy are now accepted ways of working with children and young people who are marginalized and oppressed, and independent advocacy is recognized as an essential tool for promoting their voice and agency and challenging social injustice (Boylan and Dalrymple 2006). In this chapter, we chart the development of advocacy by locating it within professional practice and consider the impact of changing perspectives concerning the advocacy role of professionals. We then go on to look at the influence of the service user movement, the emergence of independent advocacy within the four nations of the UK and the significance of international developments.

## Advocacy in professional practice

Advocacy is considered to be an essential skill for both health and social care professionals. Historically, advocacy has been a moral obligation for nurses and has traditionally been seen as a skill for social workers (Bateman 2000;

Payne 2000b; Trevithick 2000). However, in both health and social care practice changes in the delivery of services has had an impact on how far professional practitioners feel able to directly advocate for patients or service users. Furthermore, this is complicated by the fact that first and foremost professionals work to ensure that the 'best interests' of a child or young person is the paramount consideration in any decision that they make. We will therefore begin by briefly examining the constraints inherent in the concept of 'best interests' (see Box 1.1).

The Children Act 1948 placed a responsibility on local authorities when making decisions to further the 'best interests of the child'. This was later developed through the Children and Young Person's Act 1969. In the Children Act 1989, the principle for decision making set out in Section 1 (3)(a) reinforces the concept of 'best interests' and the welfare of the child, rather than embodying children's rights. The best interests of the child, however, is also a key principle set out in Article 3 of the UNCRC, which states that: 'In all actions concerning the child, whether undertaken by public or private social welfare institutions, courts of law, administrative authorities or legislative bodies, the best interests of the child shall be the primary consideration'.

It can be argued that the best interests principle is a check to ensure that professional decision makers carry out their responsibilities for the benefit of the child. However, the principle is one that has been challenging for lawyers and child care professionals as they have sought to reconcile the meaning of children's rights with the concept of 'best interests of the child': is a child or young person an autonomous decision maker who can direct his or her representation or is the child in need of a representative who would 'discover' and then advocate for what is best for them? (Spinak 2007). The work of Joseph Goldstein, Anna Freud and Albert Solnit published between 1973 and 1986 in

---

**Box 1.1**   Exercise: 'Best interests'

Think about a time when as a child or young person your parents/carers made a decision without your involvement that you were told would 'be good for you'.

How did you feel about not being involved in the decision making?
Did you understand why the decision was made?
Did you agree with it?
On reflection did you feel that the decision was in your best interest?
How do you feel now about what happened?
Has this had an impact on your understanding of the concept of best interest?
How does this influence the way that you work with children and young people and other professionals?

three volumes and republished as a single text *The Best Interests of the Child* in 1996 has been influential in informing both these debates and the development of child welfare policy in the UK and further afield. The debates centre on the fact that a decision that appears to be in the best interests of the child and a decision that the child desires may be in conflict. Recognition of the importance of child-centred practice (Parton 2006) has clearly influenced decision making and Spinak's analysis of the texts of Goldstein and his colleagues is interesting:

> Goldstein et al called on legislators and courts to ask continuously: 'Does the law reflect the current state of knowledge to minimize harm when the state intervenes in the lives of families?' I believe they would recognize today that the current state of knowledge about lawyers for children indicates that only child-directed representation is most likely to achieve that result.
>
> (Spinak 2007: 11)

Nevertheless, research indicates that tensions remain between children's welfare and children's rights, with children and young people feeling that when decisions are taken on the basis of what is perceived to be in their best interests, invariably they are not included in the decision-making process: 'Often, "best interests" doesn't involve the child, or they are not listened to, but it doesn't work if they don't engage the child in the process' (Elsa, advocate in Oliver et al. 2006: 9).

A young person who wishes to express a view that appears to be against his or her 'best interests' may involve an independent advocate to help them do this. This can cause professionals some concern and even create conflict between advocates and professionals, who may feel that the advocate is not then acting in that young person's best interest. However, it is often misunderstanding about the role of the advocate that gives rise to such conflict. The independent advocate has a specific role – to ensure that the views and perspectives of the young person are expressed – which in turn enables those responsible for making decisions in the young person's best interest to be as fully informed as possible. By helping young people to express their true feelings, advocates are therefore acting in the best interests of those young people – even when the views that they express are in conflict with the views of the professional decision makers. Understanding a young person's perspective is key to achieving outcomes that are in their best interest, since alienation of the young person from the decision-making process presents a greater risk of the desired outcomes failing. Josh's situation is interesting in this respect (Box 1.2). While arguably prolonging the decision may well have been unsettling for Josh and not in his best interests, honesty by the local authority regarding how far the issue of limited resources contributed to the

---

**Box 1.2**   'Best interests' case study: Josh

---

Josh could not accept that it was in his best interest to move placements after his sixteenth birthday. By persistently expressing this view and asking for further explanations, the authority reluctantly accepted that cost had been a significant factor in the decision, since the placement he was leaving had been a specialist placement and therefore a costly one. Once the authority had admitted this, Josh was able to accept the decision rather than fighting them further saying, 'Oh well, if they can't afford it I suppose I will have to move on'. Josh then moved to his new placement in a more positive frame of mind than he would have done had he still been expected to accept that it was in his best interests.

During this process, Josh's advocate was frequently told that she was harming him by expressing his wish to remain in his current placement and that prolonging the move was only making things harder for him. However, the persistence of Josh and his advocate led to a more honest explanation that opened the door for him to accept the decision and move on in a more positive frame of mind.

So, did advocating his views act against Josh's best interests or for them?

Expressing a view on behalf of a young person that is apparently contrary to their best interests is sometimes construed as being detrimental, as it is felt that in some way this encourages the young person not to accept a proposed course of action or to raise hopes or expectations that a decision might be changed when it will not. This view often arises out of a misunderstanding of the advocate's role. While an advocate is not there to persuade, part of the advocacy role is to assist a young person to make an informed decision and that will include discussion of the likely outcomes of various courses of action. However, as this part of the advocacy process is confidential and not observed by the professionals charged with acting in the child's best interest, it is not always understood by those outside the advocacy profession. As advocates, it is important for us to explain to agencies that assisting young people to reach informed decisions is an important part of our work, albeit that it is protected by confidentiality and so unseen by others. In the event of the young person still wishing to express a view that is contrary to that of their adult carers and professionals, it is still 'in their best interests' to express it. The important issue here is that it is an understanding of the young person's viewpoint that is crucial. This is not the same as agreeing with their viewpoint.

(Case study and commentary provided by Ruth Holgate,
Maze Advocacy Service 2006)

decision – which he clearly understood – would ultimately have also been in his best interests.

Commentators have expressed concern that changes introduced to safeguard the welfare of children and young people, that are placing them at the centre of new services, will not be child or young person centred. This is because, for professionals attempting to genuinely ensure the best interests of children and young people, there is the potential for concerns about their vulnerability to result in 'a huge explosion of activity which only tangentially relates to the concerns of children and young people themselves' (Parton 2006: 185). In a discussion about the concept of best interests, Timms (1995) points out that the 'best interests' model may produce a more punitive form of care than one that is organized around children's rights, noting that while local authorities do have their statutory responsibilities, there is also a need for professionals to treat the concept with caution, since:

> it may not always be that the local authority view and the best interests of the child are one and the same thing, although there is a prevailing fantasy to that effect which manifests itself in the assertion that any contradiction of the local authority view is, by definition, failing to give consideration to the welfare of the child.
>
> (Timms 1995: 425)

We shall see in the following examination of advocacy in professional practice that it is this concept of 'best interests' that can make it difficult for health and social care professionals in particular to always advocate for children and young people in decision-making processes. In some areas of professional work with young people, such as education, the advocacy role has been less prominent. Nevertheless, the influence of the advocacy agenda has had an impact on enabling children and young people to be involved in the planning and delivery of services and on individual decision making (Thomas 2001; Boylan and Braye 2006; Oliver and Dalrymple 2008).

The role of advocacy in *nursing* has developed over the last two decades since the UKCC (United Kingdom Central Council for Nursing, Midwifery and Health Visitors)[3] Code of Professional Conduct was issued in 1984. While this does not specifically mention advocacy, it implies the notion of advocacy in a commentary on the code (UKCC 1984) clearly indicating that the advocacy role is considered to be a key element of good professional practice. Subsequent guidelines make the notion of advocacy more obvious, noting that nurses should not act in a way that they assume is in the best interests of a patient but should ensure that they provide information to enable patients to feel confident about making their own decisions and support them once a decision has been made (UKCC 1996). In 1995, however, an occasional paper issued by the Royal College of Nurses (RCN) states very specifically that nurses can advocate on behalf of a patient and speak up for them when a programme of care is delivered. Similarly, guidance for mental health and learning disabilities nurses (UKCC 1998: 14) clearly identifies the advocacy role, stating that 'advocacy is about promoting clients' rights to choose and empowering them to decide for themselves'. An advice sheet produced by the Nursing and Midwifery Council (NMC) entitled *Advocacy and Autonomy* is equally clear and, interestingly, also identifies the need for advocacy, stating that: 'Advocacy is concerned with promoting and protecting the interests of patients/clients, many of whom may be vulnerable and incapable of protecting their own interests. They may lack the support of family and friends' (NMC 2006: 1).

Since advocacy first appeared in the nursing curriculum (UKCC 1988), however, and nursing textbooks have promoted the advocacy role, literature about 'patient advocacy' has increasingly questioned the ability of nurses to truly advocate for patients, suggesting that the obstacles inherent within work settings make it difficult for nurses to be effective advocates. While nurses may therefore have no doubt about their ethical obligation to advocate (Gates 1994; Mallick 1998), research indicates that the barriers for nurses include concern that it could harm professional relationships within healthcare settings, with nurses feeling powerless and afraid to speak out, as well as more practical time constraints (Mallick 1998; Negarandeh et al. 2006). Furthermore, commentators argue that the lack of a universally accepted definition of advocacy within nursing is also problematic (Baldwin 1993; Bennett 1999; Wheeler 2000). Without such a definition, they suggest, nurses are not recognized legally as specifically fulfilling the advocacy role and, if they do, cannot be clear about whether their interpretation of advocacy is in line with that of their professional body.

Although nursing education and guidance from professional bodies puts advocacy at the heart of professional nursing practice, there has also been increasing recognition that for several reasons this is not always possible. Guidance for mental health and learning disability nurses indicates the need for clarity for the nurse acting as advocate, particularly when professional responsibilities make it difficult to be objective. The need for nurses to be aware of independent advocacy and to support patients to access them has therefore entered the literature (Wheeler 2000), while guidance is equally clear that nurses need to 'distinguish between your professional responsibility to advocate on a client's behalf and the role of a trained independent advocate. In most instances, an independent advocate can provide more objective support to clients' (UKCC 1998: 14) .

Other health care professionals working with children and young people also have an advocacy remit. For example, the Royal College of Paediatrics and Child Health Advocacy Committee (2008: 7) have adopted an overall aim in relation to advocacy, which is '[t]o advocate the rights of children and young people in society and to promote their health needs and services'. In a comprehensive handbook, they set out a further four specific objectives (Box 1.3) that cover direct advocacy (relating to individuals or specific groups) and what they term public policy advocacy (relating to changes in systems for children and young people)[4].

The College sees paediatricians as being well placed to act as advocates because they have the power of their status – being held in high regard as respected professionals, they are highly trained and, significantly, 'they generally have no other axe to grind than the welfare of the child concerned' (Royal College of Paediatrics and Child Health Advocacy Committee 2008: 11). They see themselves as having the necessary 'clout' to ensure that children receive the services they deserve. The problem here, of course, is that this professional power can inhibit nurses and possibly other professionals from feeling able to advocate when necessary. Interestingly, however, the guidance indicates how paediatricians can use their position in a range of situations outside the health system to help individual children. Examples include giving evidence for disability or other benefit appeals, helping in child protection investigations, assisting families to obtain better housing, obtaining specialist treatment of community-based facilities and supporting claims for special education. However, as with other health and social care professionals, paediatricians acknowledge that they are not skilled advocates and neither are they independent (see Box 1.4).

In *social work*, advocacy was identified as a central skill by the first social work training body, the Central Council for Education and Training in Social Work (CCETSW 1995). It is also identified by the British Association of Social Workers (BASW 2002) as a key element of the social work role and more recently a key skill for social workers completing the social work degree[5]. Historically, advocacy in social work has a long tradition and has been an essential element of its professional codes of ethics. Payne (2000a) notes that

---

**Box 1.3** Royal College of Paediatrics and Child Health Advocacy Committee objectives

Aims:

- To ensure that the opinions of children inform the development of child health services.
- To lobby for national policies relating to the effects of poverty and disadvantage on the health of children.
- To publicize key issues relating to the health of children.
- To ensure that paediatricians have training and guidance to enable them to act as advocates.

---

**Box 1.4**   Limitations to paediatricians acting as advocates

---

Paediatricians have a responsibility to ensure that children and their families are aware that they:

- cannot guarantee to argue in favour of the child's or parents' wishes if this conflicts with their own professional judgement of the child's best interests;
- have a responsibility to other children as well. Sometimes what is good for one child, or group of children may end up disadvantaging other children. They therefore need to be careful to avoid unintended negative consequences from their advocacy;
- are not entirely independent or disinterested. Circumstances may arise where they need to consider the effects of their advocacy on relationships with professional colleagues or on the institution, or the possibility of disciplinary proceedings by senior staff;
- may not be able to devote adequate time to the child's case; and
- in *certain* circumstances they may have to breach confidentiality.

(Royal College of Paediatrics and Child Health Advocacy
Committee 2008: s. 12)

---

the only social worker to become Prime Minister, Clement Attlee, stated that social workers should be 'agitators' on behalf of their clients, while analyses of social work skills have always highlighted advocacy as a key skill and function of social work. Advocacy was widespread in the settlement movement, becoming less of a focus as 'social work practice and social work education turned their focus towards management and administrative theories, losing sight of advocacy and reform goals' (Haynes and Mickelson 1997: 11). Nevertheless, the influence of radical theorists and the development of welfare rights services led to the notion of 'principled advocacy' (Bateman 2000), which essentially means trying to get as much as possible for service users without colluding with oppressive elements of the system.

In an examination of the nature of relationships in social work, Payne (1996) has argued that intervention is undertaken through four roles: the conferee, the broker, the mediator and the advocate, the latter role involving putting the case for resources or social change on behalf of others. Haynes and Mickelson (1997) are very clear that the role of enabler or advocate is a key function of social work practitioners, describing the role in terms of helping clients to become independent from service providers and in the process developing the skills to advocate for themselves. The broker/advocate role has also been described as linking people with resources or acting as an intermediary – the social broker advocate and the community organizing advocate (Dubois and Krogsrund Miley 1992). However, Johnson (1989) argues that the roles of broker and advocate should not be confused, defining the broker role as helping to get needed services (including assessing a situation, knowing alternative services, preparing and counselling the person, contacting the appropriate services and ensuring that the person gets to the help and uses it). The advocate, on the other hand, supports or speaks on behalf of someone to find different interpretations or exceptions to regulations and procedures, emphasizing rights to services and highlighting situations where people are not receiving or using services.

Reflecting on confusion about the language of advocacy, Bull suggests that a British working party missed an opportunity to fully understand the term in their consideration of the role and tasks of social workers (Barclay Report 1982):

> Alas, the working party recklessly littered its report with references to 'advice', 'advocacy', 'brokerage', 'mediation', and 'negotiation'. Sometimes, two or more of these were used interchangeably; once or twice they were loosely distinguished, but never were they adequately defined and delineated.
>
> (Bull 1989: 53)

We can see here that determining the role of advocacy in social work appears to be as difficult as articulating the concept within nursing. Essentially, the debates are around 'advocacy as activity' and 'advocacy as role' (McCall 1978: 208), or in the language of social work education, advocacy as a social work method and advocacy as a social work skill. The literature indicates that social workers and other professionals in health and social care can and should include advocacy as part of their required repertoire of skills. Other conflicting roles create tensions, however, and there will therefore be times when people need an independent advocate (Brandon 1995; Clifton and Hodgson 1997; Downs et al. 1997; Oliver and Dalrymple 2008). Furthermore, just as the rapidly changing nature of social work and welfare provision is likely to have an impact on the development of social work values and professional ethics (Shardlow 2001), it is also likely to influence these professionals' advocacy role. The managerialism that currently pervades the provision of services has the potential, it is argued, to deny democratic arguments for advocacy and participation.

Within Children's Services, social workers have a central role in listening to, understanding and responding to the views of children and young people they are working with and promoting their involvement in decision-making processes. However, there are limitations to their capacity to act as advocates (Dalrymple 1995; Boylan and Boylan 1998; Pithouse et al. 2005). They face similar dilemmas to medical professionals when their independence is compromised by their role as the provider of services. For example, they may come under pressure from managers to allocate scarce resources in a particular way, determined by available resources rather than underpinned by a needs-led assessment. Equally, social workers, like other professionals working with young people, may fear the consequences of challenging the policy and practice of their employing authority: 'Workers have to be mindful of the fact that they are employees and those who exhibit a willingness to stand up on behalf of people they serve, frequently find themselves in trouble with the employing body' (Kennedy 1990: 32).

Social workers share with nurses, paediatricians and other health professionals the dilemmas of working within the 'best interests' principle that underpins their decision making and practice. Holding powerful positions in relation to young people, their capacity to advocate on behalf of children and young people they are working with is invariably limited (Barford and Wattam 1991). Increasing recognition of these dilemmas, coupled with the findings of a succession of enquiry reports (Levy and Kahan 1991; Utting 1991, 1997; Waterhouse et al. 2000), means that it is now acknowledged that particular groups of children and young people should have access to independent forms of advocacy. This provides a potential mechanism to promote young people's active participation in decision-making processes. While independent advocacy is not a panacea, it endeavours to overcome the possible conflicts of interest that can arise through being part of the system of services for children and young people. However, research indicates a level of ambivalence in relation to the involvement of independent advocates (Pithouse et al. 2005; Oliver et al. 2006) indicating that, despite policy, legislation and guidance, there is still some way to go:

> Some professionals have welcomed and encouraged the involvement of an advocate with a young person. However, others perceive a young person accessing an advocate as a threat, 'creating problems that previously did not exist'.
>
>                                             (Boylan and Boylan 1998: 47)

Barriers

> There are lots of different social work teams in the area and they are all quite different. The relationship is down to the perception of the social worker and how positively they view advocacy. Also, some specific cases can be challenging, especially about individual practice.
>
>                      (Linda, advocacy service manager in Oliver 2008: 35)

In *education*, there is an increasing engagement with the need to both support children's and young people's learning throughout the education system, and encourage their involvement in the 'life of the school'. This may take the form of school buddies, prefects, coaches and mentors, schools councils and, of course, through formal and informal relationships with teaching and mentoring staff working with children and young people. Fielding also notes the development of:

> more innovative, often student-led developments (e.g. school ambassadors, student-led learning walks, lead learners, student leaders, student co-researchers and lead researchers, and more radical forms of student council), to a burgeoning range of ways in which professional perceptions about the suitability and performance of staff are significantly informed by the student perspective.
>
> (Fielding 2006: 1)

However, Fielding's commentary indicates that the 'new wave' student voice through 'multiple managed opportunities for teachers to listen to young people's views' (p. 6) does not necessarily demonstrate a commitment to what he calls 'person-centred' learning communities.

Shier (2006) suggests that the emphasis by teachers on the need to maintain authority – effectively maintaining control over students – is one explanation for the lack of participatory practice in decision making. Shier, in his work with a locally run rural community education organization supporting child workers in the coffee industry in Nicaragua, promotes the notion of partnership working between learners and educators encouraging the empowerment of students as a positive move forward rather than a challenge to the traditional authority of teachers. However, while government guidance on hearings considering the exclusion of children and young people from school indicates a commitment to their involvement in this individual decision-making process, in some ways exclusion may often be a response to challenges to authority. Nevertheless, the guidance does state that young people should be allowed to express their views unless there is good reason to the contrary (DfEE 1999). However, there are concerns that children are unable to express their views and have them taken seriously within the education system in the UK – in contrast to the majority of children and young people in education in the rest of Europe. For example:

- children and young people are not allowed to sit on governing bodies;
- parents have the right of appeal against a permanent school exclusion but there is no such right for the child or young person involved in the process;
- there is no system to challenge injustice, discrimination or abuse;
- there is no mechanism for consultation in relation to issues such as the National Curriculum, teaching methods or school policies.

Although the development of school councils[6] offers the potential for progressive practice, as with many participatory initiatives the way that they are set up and facilitated will influence how far the children and young people involved are able to have any meaningful impact on the school or the students (Taylor with Johnson 2002). Both the UNCRC and the Crick Report on Education for Citizenship and Teaching of Democracy in Schools (Crick 1998) promote an approach that gives greater prominence to the right of children and young people as citizens. Children and young people are expected by the end of compulsory schooling to have an understanding of such concepts as equality, power, freedom and authority, as well as legal and moral rights and responsibility. Furthermore, by the end of Key Stage 3 pupils are expected to have an appropriate knowledge and understanding of the UNCRC, 'particularly the right to be heard' and have an awareness of the European Convention on Human Rights (ECHR). The Qualifications and Curriculum Authority (QCA) outlines six groups of skills that it considers are essential to enable children and young people to move into adulthood as confident and capable, one of which is that they are effective participators. This means that they need to 'play a full part in the life of their school, college, workplace or wider community by taking responsible action to bring improvements for others as well as themselves' (QCA 2007: 2). Citizenship education in schools is part of the process by which children actively claim their rights and the Crick Report regards teachers as key players in this process. However, alongside the ideal of greater prominence of student voice and participation, is a pressure on schools to 'perform' well through demonstrable outcomes and meeting of targets (Ball 2003). In addition to the challenges of children and young people with diverse needs, Fielding (2006) notes that in some contexts the level of importance given to student voice depends on the extent to which it supports wider organizational imperatives. Certainly, the view perpetuated by government agendas appears be that 'education is something that adults do to or for children and young people' (Lansdown 2001: 96).

There is an increased awareness of the experiences of those children and young people who feel marginalized and disenfranchised from education. The educational attainment of some groups of children such as working-class white males and children from some minority ethnic groups such as gypsy/traveller children and black and Asian children are notably below the national average. The rates of children excluded from school are particularly high for children from black and minority ethnic groups and children with special educational needs. Children in custody in England and Wales are excluded from the statutory right to education under Section 562 of the Education Act 1996 despite the fact that the government has been urged to address this issue by the UN Committee (Save the Children 2007).

The rights of children and young people to freely express their views and opinions is especially important when things go wrong or they feel that they have no where to turn. The Children Act 1989 placed a duty on local authorities in England and Wales to establish a representation and complaints procedure for looked after children and children in need. Section 53 of the Children Act 2004 amends Section 17 of the Children Act 1989, placing a duty on local authorities in England and Wales to ascertain children's wishes and feelings and give due consideration to them before determining what services they are entitled to, while Section 52 places duty on local authorities to promote looked after children's educational achievement. This legislation therefore applies to educational settings, with an emphasis on all children's services needing to work together to address the five outcomes that have been identified as important for children and young people: to be healthy, stay safe, enjoy and achieve, make a positive contribution and achieve economic well-being. Research is limited, but Crowley and Pithouse (2008) note that a significant number of local education authorities in Wales have, for example, no designated complaints officer and limited or no provision to ensure that marginalized children such as disabled children and ethnic minority and traveller children were able to access the complaints procedure.

The need for children and young people to access independent advocacy across health, education and social work services has been recognized (Crowley and Pithouse 2008). This has led to the emergence of independent advocacy services in the UK for children and young people in schools and educational settings, often commissioned through Children and Young People's Partnerships. Crowley (2006) points out that while the commissioning of advocacy services for children and young people is established in areas such as health and social care, progress in education has been slow. Advocacy provision has, historically, tended to respond to the needs of parents and carers trying to negotiate the complex education system, notably parents and carers of children with special educational needs. For example, the National Autistic Society Advocacy for Education Service supports parents by providing advice, information and guidance in relation to children's and young people's rights and entitlements. Parents are also supported who may be in dispute with their local authority regarding service provision, with access to an education advice line and a tribunal support scheme. However, the Special Educational Needs Code of Practice (DfES 2001a) does begin to move the emphasis towards young people by suggesting that adults can encourage self-advocacy by responding to children's messages and also recognizes that children may need advocacy support in the transitions planning process.

## The impact of service user movements

The development of service user movements as a reaction to their negative experience of welfarist and professional responses is significant in the development of advocacy. The pioneering 'in care' group, the National Association of Young People In Care (NAYPIC), established in 1979, has been important in the tradition of service user activism of establishing that children and young people should have more influence over their care and treatment and the environments in which they take place. The aims of the organization (set out in Box 5.4 in Chapter 5) emphasize its advocacy aims at both an individual and a systemic level. Until 1995, NAYPIC was a thriving organization run by young people in care for young people in care. It played a critical role in revealing and challenging poor practice in residential care. For example, studying the cases of 50 children and young people who had contacted NAYPIC over a period of three months, the organization found that over three-quarters reported physical abuse and two-thirds physical abuse (Moss et al. 1990). From their investigations of the allegations of the abuse of looked after young people, they submitted evidence to a number of inquiries into the abuse of children in residential care as well as to the Wagner Working Group on Residential Care (Wagner 1998).

Although NAYPIC did not survive in England, in Wales Voices from Care has its origins in the original organization. NAYPIC Cymru was established in 1990 as a separate group after NAYPIC began to hear from young people about their abuse in care during the late 1980s. Since there were residential homes and schools in Wales where abuse had been taking place, young people in Wales felt that they would like an organization specifically for young people living in the Welsh care system. NAYPIC Cymru went on to look into allegations of abuse in Ty Mawr Children's Home Gwent and, following an inquiry, closure of the home was recommended. NAYPIC Cymru continued to develop and changed its name to Voices from Care in 1993. Voices from Care has continued to be a campaigning organization offering training and undertaking research as well as providing advocacy and support for individual children and young people – offering one of the most confidential services in the UK. Its stated aim is to create opportunities for all young people who are or have been looked after in Wales, to have a say about the issues that are important to them.

In England, NAYPIC's replacement, A National Voice (ANV), was set up with money from the Department for Education and Skills in 1998. It became a freestanding independent company in 2006 and is managed by children and young people in care. Reflecting on the journey of this organization, one of ANV's young directors sums up the impact of the organization:

> ANV challenges and changes people's beliefs. Often a lot of people go through the care system saying, 'well this is just how it is and we have to accept it'. There is a group here who are saying that you don't have to accept it, it's not right and something must and can be done.
>
> (Jonny Hoyle, in Farrow 2006: 7)

The aim of ANV is to hear the voice of young people from care so as to make positive changes in the care system (see Box 1.5). It does not claim to be an advocacy service but its work does equate to peer advocacy[7] and systemic advocacy[8], as it organizes regular group forums and events for young people and works alongside the Department for Education and Skills, local authorities and a range of organizations for children and young people to improve systems for looked after children and young people.

---

**Box 1.5**   Aims of A National Voice

A National Voice aims:

- to continue to be a young person led organisation
- to give an individual and collective voice and to ensure young people from care have a say in all decisions that affect them
- to inform and influence central and local government decisions about the care system in England
- to educate professionals and general public about the lives and experiences of young people from care
- to promote positive images of young people from care
- to raise awareness about care issues and reduce stigma to positively promote the rights of young people from care and to promote the United Nations Convention on the Rights of the Child

What it does is:

- help young people from all over England to set up and join in local in-care/ aftercare groups
- help young people change the care system for the better
- help young people speak up and have an effect on decisions about the care system
- help young people send out good messages about themselves and tackle any bad ones

(www.anationalvoice.org)

---

## The impetus for contemporary advocacy: UK perspectives

Ratification by the UK in 1991 of the United Nations Convention on the Rights of the Child (1989) provided an opportunity to promote a perspective of children and young people as active citizens with the capacity to participate in the public arena. However, debates about children's rights have developed within a protection/liberation continuum (Franklin 1986; Lindsay 1992; Jenkins 1995), which is reflected in the 'faltering and uneven' (Franklin 2002) progress in achieving rights for children. Consequently, development of advocacy services for children and young people throughout all four nations of the UK has been described as inconsistent and fragmented.

In England and Wales, the UNCRC had an impact on the Children Act 1989, which created a new agenda for child care practice (Denney 1998) and provided 'a fresh impetus' for children to be involved in decision making processes' (Cloke and Davies 1995: xiv). The Act was seen as a progressive piece of legislation, being described as 'the most far-reaching reform of child care law which has come before Parliament in living memory' (Lord Mackay 1988, *Hansard* H.L. Vol. 502, col. 488) and interpreted as a vehicle for empowering children and young people (Smith and Woodhead 1999). Both the Children Act 1989 and the regulations and guidance stress the importance of ascertaining the child's wishes and feelings (in the light of their age and understanding) and involving children throughout the decision-making process.

Bainham suggests that 'the message of the modern law is that the capacity of children of all ages to express a valid opinion on matters affecting them must not be underestimated' (Bainham 2005: 139). However, it is worth noting that there had been a requirement to consider the child's wishes and feelings in both the Children Act 1975 and in Section 18 of the Child Care Act 1980. Essentially, the Children Act 1989 in England and Wales, the Children (Scotland) Act 1995 and the Children (Northern Ireland) Order 1995 brought the requirement to consider the wishes and feelings of the child to the fore. However, how far the legislation does provide a satisfactory framework for children's rights is contested (Roche 2002). In many respects, the Children Act 1989 only partially secured the participation rights of children and young people, and then only when things go wrong (Willow 1998). While its central principles encourage partnership practice with both parents and young people, and the Act widened the responsibilities of social workers, Parton (1999, 2006) argues that this piece of legislation is primarily concerned to manage risk, practitioners focusing on making defensible decisions and making them more accountable to the courts.

A significant element both of the Children Act 1989 and the National

Health Service and Community Care Act 1990 was the introduction of statutory complaints procedures, enabling children as consumers the statutory right to question decisions. For children and young people, however, Timms (1995) notes that the reactions of adults to complaints made by children indicate the need for them to have access to independent advocacy, since:

- The problem may be denied on the basis that the child has misunderstood or over-reacted.
- The complaint may be explained away as a function of the child or young person's problem; for example she or he is seen as attention seeking.
- Attempts may be made to undermine the credibility of the advocates themselves. Listening to the child or young person rather than the professionals, who have a statutory responsibility to pursue the courses of action which will be in the child's best interests, may be experienced as deeply threatening by the workers involved.

(Timms 1995: 373)

Furthermore, research indicates that for children and young people making a complaint is far from easy. They find complaints procedures both difficult to access and intimidating to use (Aiers and Kettle 1998; Wallis and Frost 1998; Waterhouse et al. 2000; Payne and Pithouse 2006; Pithouse and Crowley 2006). Clearly, children and young people who want to make a complaint are in a vulnerable position and the development of advocacy as a way of supporting them to do this was a driving force in establishing advocacy services in the early 1990s. This historic link between advocacy and complaints has possibly led to a somewhat tense relationship between independent advocates and other professionals involved in the lives of children and young people (Wattam and Parton 1999; Payne 2000a; Goldson 2001; Boylan and Ing 2005) This can also be seen in more recent research concerning advocacy and complaints in Wales:

> it seemed evident that in some authorities there was a reluctance by social work teams to meet with advocates and make referrals. This stemmed from a culture of mistrust and a belief that advocacy 'creates complaints' and undermined practitioner attempts to control risks and pursue organisational and protectionist agendas.
>
> (Pithouse and Crowley 2008: 143)

Research and inquiries following implementation of the Children Act 1989 indicate that children's and young people's participation is still difficult in adult-led decision-making processes such as reviews (Boylan and Ing 2005; Boylan 2008) or child protection conferences (Farnfield 1997; Boylan and Wylie 1999; Dalrymple and Horan 2008a). Even in more progressive participatory decision-making forums such as Family Group Conferences, children and young people do not always feel that they are heard (Dalrymple 2007; Laws and Kirby 2007). Nevertheless, service user involvement and empowerment practice since the late 1980s have led to what Beresford and Croft (2000) describe as the 'emergence of new participants in social policy: service users and their movements', while the election of New Labour in 1997 and their Third Way agenda led to a rapid expansion of legislative mandates for advocacy for a range of service users. For example, in England the White Paper 'Valuing People' (Department of Health 2001) relating to people with learning difficulties promotes the concept of advocacy, while the Mental Capacity Act 2005 makes it a statutory duty for people who lack the capacity to make decisions to be supported by an Independent Mental Capacity Advocate (IMCA)[9]. For children and young people, initiatives such as Quality Protects[10] in England and Children First in Wales have been significant, while guidelines for safeguarding children (Department of Health, Home Office and Department for Education and Employment 1999; National Assembly for Wales 2000) indicate that advocacy and the participation of children and young people in decision making is being given a high priority: 'Children and families may be supported in the safeguarding process by advice and advocacy services, and they should always be informed of services which exist, both locally and nationally' (Department of Health 2006a, para. 10.5).

Two significant landmarks can be identified in the establishment of independent advocacy in England and Wales. In England, the appointment of Mike Lindsay in 1987 as the first UK Children's Rights Officer was an important turning point in recognizing the participation rights of children and young people who were looked after in local authority care. He set up a children's rights service to educate children and staff about the rights of looked after children in Leicester. He also made himself available as an advocate to take up issues on behalf of individual children or young people. Through working in this way his service was pro-active and he was able to help young people sort out problems before they became a complaint. He established a model for good advocacy practice by being both educative and adversarial (James 1992). The second landmark, in 1992, was the development of the first national advocacy service covering England and Wales. Two well-established voluntary organizations came together to set up a new organization called ASC (Advice, Advocacy and Representation Services for Children, now NYAS, National Youth Advocacy Service). The two organizations had considerable experience of pioneering rights based services for children and young people. VCC (A Voice for the Child in Care, now called VOICE) was the organization that developed independent representation for children and young people in secure accommodation. They also developed an advocacy service for children and young people in the care of the London Borough of Greenwich. The second organization, IRCHIN (Independent Representation for Children in

Need), pioneered independent representation in complaints procedures and independent court reports for children involved in care proceedings, which developed into an organization for guardians ad litem[11]. It also ran a pilot complaints and advocacy scheme for children looked after in residential homes run by National Children's Homes (NCH). ASC worked in association with ChildLine, which operated a freephone line specifically set up for looked after children. The service was supported through initial funding by the Department of Health, which was supplemented by charitable funding to provide a confidential independent service.

Children's rights and advocacy services have since been set up by all local authorities in England and throughout Wales. Most supplied through voluntary sector providers that vary in how they are staffed and managed. However, the identification of independent advocacy as a crucial support mechanism for children and young people wishing to use formal complaints procedures has resulted in legislative mandates for children and young people's advocacy. In response to the Waterhouse Report, a Children's Commissioner was appointed in Wales in 2000, the first such Commissioner in the UK, while changes to the Children Act 1989, introduced through the Adoption and Children Act 2002, gave looked after children and young people and care leavers making or intending to make a complaint under the Children Act 1989 a statutory right to advocacy. In addition, the governments of England and Wales have published guidance to advocacy service providers through National Standards for the Provision of Advocacy (Department of Health 2002; Welsh Assembly Government 2003), which are informed by the UNCRC and set out what children and young people can expect from advocacy services.

The first national study of advocacy for children and young people in England, funded by the Department of Health, was undertaken in 2004 (Oliver et al. 2005, 2006), while in Wales the Children's Commissioner published a report in 2003 looking at the provision of advocacy services in Wales (Clarke 2003) and the Welsh Assembly Government commissioned a review of children's independent advocacy services with reference to their involvement in complaints, which was published in 2005 (Pithouse et al. 2005). These indicated that in both England and Wales independent advocacy services are currently generally commissioned by local authorities through service level agreements with national or voluntary organizations, although in England just under one-quarter (23%) are provided directly by the local authority. Most are targeted at specific groups of young people (for example, primarily looked after young people, care leavers, children in need and young people in reviews, case conferences or family group conferences) and seem to vary in terms of accessibility, quality and stability.

Proposals to improve access to advocacy by the respective governments in England and Wales are ongoing and controversial. In England, the Green Paper 'Every Child Matters' (2003) suggested that all looked after children and young people should have three key individuals in their lives – a social worker, a carer (residential or foster carer) and an independent advocate. However, in attempting to introduce the advocacy element, the paper confused the roles of independent visitor and independent advocate. An independent visitor is a volunteer who provides a long-term befriending service to a young person (Children Act 1989[12]). Although a crucial role, it is nevertheless very different to the professional role of an independent advocate. While acknowledging that this misguided move was confusing and diluted the two roles and recognizing that children and young people feel that they should have access to a champion or advocate, the subsequent White Paper 'Care Matters: Time for Change' (DfES 2007) did not provide a statutory right for children and young people to have access to independent advocacy when significant decisions are being made about their lives. Proposals in the Children and Young Persons Bill did extend the role of independent reviewing officers (IROs)[13] (who chair the statutory reviews of all looked after children).

However, in a memorandum on behalf of the Children's Advocacy Consortium, two organizations – Voice and the Children's Society – pointed out that the primary remit of IROs to act in the best interests of the child conflicts with any advocacy role. The argument against an IRO taking on the advocacy role includes recognition that the responsibilities inherent in chairing review meetings means that IROs are unable to provide the necessary dedicated support to children and young people to ensure that their views are clearly represented. The memorandum made the crucial observation that an advocate can question people attending a review in a way that is not possible from the position of a chairperson. When the Bill subsequently went through the Commons Committee stage, assurances were made that IROs would be required to give information about advocacy to the child and seek the assistance of a professional independent advocate if they are unable to ascertain the wishes and feelings of a child or young person.

The need for change in the way that children and young people are supported generally has been recognized in developments in the provision of advocacy services in Wales. The Welsh Assembly Government has been proactive in promoting advocacy for children and young people in Wales, setting up an Advocacy Unit to establish advocacy nationally. Following consultation on a major reorganization to deliver a matrix of children's rights, advocacy and participation services across public services (Welsh Assembly Government 2007), the Welsh Assembly Government put forward a proposal to commission advocacy regionally through a consortia of local authorities, health trust and their partners. The final service framework for the provision of advocacy in Wales is led by a National Independent Advocacy Board, supported by an Advocacy Development and Performance Unit set up within the Assembly Government. The role of the Unit is to commission, manage and monitor an Advocacy and Advice Service across Wales. There are two elements to the service: a single point of contact provided through the National Advocacy and Advice Service for all young people and a locally/regionally commissioned Integrated Specialist Advocacy Service across health, social care and education services to provide what they term statutory advocacy and broader support for vulnerable children and young people (Children and Young People Committee 2008; Hutt 2008). Writing at the time of the initial consultation, Pithouse and Crowley note that in Wales, 'what is clear is that advocacy and children's rights are prominently on the policy agenda in Wales at the moment and significant change of some kind seems inescapable' (Pithouse and Crowley 2008: 147).

In Scotland, the promotion of children's rights within the youth justice system has been unique through the development of the Children's Hearings System. This pioneering way of working with children and young people who offend was based on the vision of Lord Kilbrandon set out in the Kilbranadon Report (1964) and implemented through the Social Work (Scotland) Act 1968. The system was designed to bring together the law, expertise in the provision of child care and informed lay judgement so that decisions can be made on what care is in the best interests of a particular child. It is underpinned by the key principle that children who offend and children in need of care and protection should be dealt with in the same system – essentially a system that is centred on the welfare of the child. An independent panel of trained lay people consider situations regarding children where compulsory measures of intervention may be needed. The panel makes decisions relating to a child's welfare and the courts deal with disputed facts and any appeals. The rights of children and parents are protected by the legal framework.

In 2006, the Scottish Executive commissioned a review of the Children's Hearings System 'Getting it Right for Every Child' (Scottish Executive 2006). As part of that review, a research project was undertaken to establish how advocacy for children in the Children's Hearings System compared with arrangements in other UK systems of child welfare and youth justice and internationally. The aim of the research was to find out what children and young people and professionals working with them thought about advocacy arrangements within the system and how they could be improved (Creegan et al. 2006). The researchers developed a definition of advocacy that they felt reflected the complexity of the options available to enable children and young people to understand, communicate and participate effectively according to their age and understanding in hearings processes and in important decisions which affect their lives:

> At its broadest, advocacy is the provision of information, explanations, support, simple encouragement to participate, or direct advocacy by way of representation. Children and young people involved

in the Children's Hearings System experience a need for a mixture of these things at different stages in their involvement with the System and to differing degrees depending on their particular needs.

(Creegan et al. 2006: 1)

The researchers found that that despite the *implicit* commitment to providing advocacy for children and young people in the Hearings System, there was considerable variation in the extent to which it was made *explicit*. The study clearly indicated the need for independent advocacy in particular situations, while acknowledging that advocacy support might best be provided by a combination of people already involved in working with children and young people (including independent advocates). The need to achieve a balance between a common approach to providing advocacy support in hearings and a personal approach that meets the needs of individual children and young people was recognized. The researchers concluded, therefore, that a flexible but consistent approach to the provision of advocacy is needed with minimum standards. However, they make the important distinction between advocacy, best interests and the active participation of children and young people in decision making. Prior to this research, a report about child abuse in the Western Isles had made a recommendation about advocacy support for all children involved in meetings involving decisions about their care needs and protection. However, the focus of an advocate envisaged here was to promote the best interests of the child or young person. In contrast, the research for Getting it Right for Every Child identified that the role of an advocate in the Hearings System should not be to promote their best interests but should be to ensure the active participation of children and young people in the decision-making process.

The recommendations from the Scottish research propose a *common advocacy standard* rather than a national standard of advocacy. By this the researchers suggest that all agencies that are working with children and young people in the Hearings System will have a shared understanding of advocacy and how it relates to participation in children's hearings. They suggest that such a standard could provide a working definition of advocacy and explain how this could best be provided by agencies. In addition, they argue for a *personal advocacy plan* reflecting the circumstances, needs and wishes of a young person and taking into account support that the young person already has. Not only would this then identify any gaps in the provision of advocacy support for an individual person, but would also mean that all those involved in the process would understand the advocacy role. This is especially pertinent in view of the fact that, as discussed above, there will invariably be a number of people and agencies involved with a young person at any one time and it is important that everyone is clear about who is ensuring that the young person fully participates in the process. As the report points out:

> While advocacy support may best be provided by a combination of those already involved in supporting, and working with children and young people, including independent advocates, there will be occasions where a gap in provision needs to be met by working with a particular professional or by providing an independent advocate.
>
> (Creegan et al. 2006: 6)

In contrast to this, in a debate about the Children and Young Person's Bill (relating to England and Wales) in the House of Lords, Baroness Walmsley noted that an independent reviewing officer[14] is not the best placed to promote the views of a child or young person. She argued that there is a distinction between an IRO who is responsible for facilitating the outcomes of the decision-making process enabling the expression of a child or young person's views and the support of advocate who is independent of the process (www.theyworkforyou.com; Hansard HL Deb, 17 March 2008, c79).

As in the other nations of the UK, the development of advocacy in Northern Ireland has been fragmented. This is partly due to the fact that from 1968 it was a country in conflict and until 2007 was governed by the British Government. An impact of the conflict has been that there is still a long way to go to ensure the realization of children's rights under the UNCRC (UK Children's Commissioners 2008). Research in 2001 into the use of the Health and Personal Social Services Complaints System (Cousins et al. 2003) and a review of advocacy services for disabled children and young people (Kilkelly et al. 2008) indicates that the level and range of advocacy services vary. Furthermore, a report in 2004 indicated that independent advice, advocacy and representation services were under-developed in Northern Ireland (Kilkelly et al. 2008).

In the Republic of Ireland the picture is similar. Here is has been noted that the 'spirit of advocacy' is apparent in many policy reports and, in relation to children and young people, a report entitled 'Our Children Their Lives' (Department of Health and Children 2000) indicated that young people's participation as active citizens needed to be supported by, among other things, an advocacy process for children and young people at all levels. Arguably, this applies in all four nations of the UK.

## The impetus for advocacy through Children's Commissioners

Increasing bureaucracies in the delivery of services to children and young people allied with constraints on resources means that the question now being addressed both in the UK and beyond is: 'Whom can children turn to when the bureaucracy fails?' (Molander 1996: 576). Many countries have a clear mandate to address both individual and structural issues in this respect.

Norway took the lead by creating the first Ombudsman for Children, which 'gave official recognition to the necessity and legitimacy of child advocacy' (Flekkoy 1995: 181). Appointed in 1981, Malfrid Grude Flekkoy, the first holder of this post, described her position as 'a national defender and public conscience arouser on behalf of children' (Flekkoy 1988: 41). For her, advocacy should encompass:

> A strategy aimed at changing social systems, institutions, and structures in order to maximise children's possibilities of self determination. Child Advocacy actually has to do with a state of mind or attitude characterised by a faith in the competence of children.
>
> (Flekkoy 1988: 246)

Key to the success of advocacy, for Flekkoy, is for it to have 'some kind of public authority recognition' (Flekkoy 1991: 205). The role of the Commissioner in Norway is to protect the rights of children under the age of 19. While having no executive authority, both legally and via instruction, the Commissioner is responsible for disseminating information about children and young people and for protecting their interests. Flekkoy stated that she had to 'keep an eye on all areas of society, give warning of developments harmful to children and propose changes to improve their conditions' (Flekkoy 1991: 24).

Since the appointment of the first Children's Ombudsman there has been a steady increase in the number of ombudsmen and Children's Rights Commissioners. Sweden established a Commissioner for Children in 1985. However, the role of this Children's Ombudsman differs from the Norwegian model in a number of ways, including the fact that the post is made up of a number of workers with designated responsibility for specific areas of children's lives, such as looked after children (Ronstrom 1989). In Finland, the ombudsman works with parts of government, but remains independent, forming part of a large non-government organization. The role of the Finnish ombudsman aims to promote and defend children's rights. This is achieved in a number of ways, including the provision of legal advocacy in individual cases, raising the profile of children's rights through the dissemination of information, and training events highlighting the shortcomings of current legal and policy processes (Molander 1996). However, while commissioners' offices have since been set up in many countries throughout the world, the Norwegian model continues to be recognized as one of the pre-eminent models. Independent evaluations of the commissioners' offices in Norway and in Sweden have shown that the Commissioner is well-known and that as a result there have been positive changes in the lives of children. The work of the Norweigan Commissioner has clearly also raised the status of children and young people both in Norway and internationally.

The need for independent Children's Commissioners has been recognized throughout the UK. Wales was the first nation to set up an office with a Commissioner in post in March 2001. The Welsh Commissioner has more powers than the Commissioner in Norway, partly because it was established as a response to recommendations of an inquiry into the organized abuse of children in local authority care in North Wales. The Welsh Commissioner can review proposed legislation and policy from the National Assembly for Wales in order to consider the effect it might have on children and can make representations to the Assembly on any matters affecting them. In Ireland and Scotland, legislation has also been enacted to create Independent Children's Commissioners, the first in Northern Ireland being appointed in 2003 and in Scotland in 2004. However, in England the government was criticized for failing to appoint a Commissioner by claiming that other mechanisms exist to protect the rights of children. A group supported by over 120 organizations campaigned for a Commissioner for England, arguing that while special posts within government structures were vital and a welcome step forward, they could not meet the level of independence from government that is necessary for a commissioner to be effective (Children's Rights Alliance for England 2003). A Commissioner was eventually appointed in England in July 2005. However, the Children's Commissioners across the four nations have expressed concern that none of the offices fully complies with the characteristics of human rights institutions set out by the UN Committee on the Rights of the Child. While they have worked together to forestall any tensions arising between them, they note that the variance in their mandates, level of independence and funding arrangements could lead to tensions between them and, from the point of view of children and young people, there is an imperative for all of the Commissioners in the UK to have the capacity to promote and protect their rights (UK Children's Commissioners 2008).

Commissioners across Europe and throughout the world use the UNCRC as the framework for their work. Despite the fact that they exist in different legal structures and have varying roles, Commissioners have achieved a great deal for children and young people, including promoting reforms in law, highlighting discrimination of vulnerable groups, increasing knowledge, and understanding about children's rights and advocating the views of children and young people (Children's Rights Alliance for England 2003). The European network of Ombudspeople for Children publishes annual assessments of the work of twenty institutions, indicating that the appointment of Commissioners clearly creates a climate of respect for children and young people, which in turn enhances their status and enables them to come to voice.

---

**Box 1.6**  Children's Commissioners in the four nations of the UK

---

WALES

The Children's Commissioner for Wales was the first to be established in the UK, under the provisions of the Care Standards Act 2000. The Commissioner's role was extended to cover all children by the Children's Commissioner for Wales Act 2001.The first Commissioner, Peter Clarke, took office in 2001. In addition to the general functions of Commissioners[15], the Welsh Commissioner's functions include: monitoring and reviewing arrangements made by care providers in relation to complaints, whistle-blowing, advice/support and advocacy. The Welsh Commissioner has powers of independent investigation and is not required to consult with the Secretary of State beforehand. The Children's Commissioner for Wales Regulations[16] require the Commissioner in the exercise of his or her functions to have regard to the UNCRC.

NORTHERN IRELAND

The Commissioner for Children and Young People for Northern Ireland took office in 2003 under the provisions of the Children and Young People (Northern Ireland) Order 2003. Nigel Williams took office in 2003. The Commissioner's remit[17] includes, 'safeguarding and promoting the rights and best interests of children'[18]. Like the Welsh Commissioner, the Northern Ireland Commissioner has the power to hold an independent inquiry without consulting the Secretary of State. Duties include promoting an awareness of children's rights. The powers of the Northern Ireland Commissioner are similar to those of the Welsh Commissioner regarding whistle-blowing, monitoring and reviewing. The Commissioner, in the exercise of his or her functions, is to have regard to the UNCRC[19].

SCOTLAND

The first Scottish Commissioner for Children and Young People, Kathleen Marshall, took office in 2004, under the provisions of the Commissioner for Children and Young People (Scotland) Act 2003.The functions of the Commissioner include promoting and safeguarding children's rights[20], promoting awareness of children's rights, and reviewing law and policy relating to children's rights. The Scottish Commissioner does not have the power to carry out investigations into particular children (unlike the Welsh and Northern Ireland Commissioners). The Commissioner is not required to consult with the Secretary of State before holding an independent inquiry. The Scottish Commissioner is required, in exercising his or her functions, to have regard to the UNCRC[21].

Continued

---

**Box 1.6**   Continued

---

ENGLAND

The Children's Commissioner for England, Al Aynsley-Green, took office in 2005 under the provisions of the Children Act 2004. The functions of the English Commissioner are set out in Section 2 (i) of the Children Act 2004 and the Commissioner's general function is restrictive – 'promoting awareness of the views and interests of children in England' as they relate to five stated indicators of children's well-being[22]. Other functions include 'advising the Secretary of State on the views and interests of children[23] and ensuring they inform the policy process.

The Commissioner has the power to investigate individual children's cases, if they raise issues 'of public policy relevance' to all children. Unlike any of the other Commissioners in the UK, the English Commissioner must consult with the Secretary of State before holding an independent inquiry. The Commissioner must have regard to the UNCRC in consideration of the interests of children.

---

## Summary

We have charted the development of advocacy through an examination of the advocacy role of professionals and a survey of current practice around the four nations of the UK. The advocacy role of professionals can be constrained both by policy imperatives and by the concept of 'best interests'. While child care professionals can and do use advocacy skills in their daily work, the development of advocacy services for children and young people in the UK has been a response to the need to promote their participatory rights in decision making. Advocacy has become established against a background of competing views about childhood, with varying perspectives on children's rights, which will be explored further in the following chapters. Nevertheless, children and young people have clearly identified their need to have access to independent advocacy to enable them to have more influence over their own lives. Governments in the UK also recognize the need for children and young people to have a voice and the development of a range of advocacy services is testament to that fact. In other European countries, the development of Children's Commissioners provides the necessary institutions to promote and protect the rights of children and young people and ensure that they have a direct impact on the institutions that affect their lives.

## Notes

1 Frost and Stein (1989) cite child paupers in workhouses under the Poor Law as an example.

2 Al Aynsley-Green was appointed as the first Children's Commissioner in England in 2005.

3 The UKCC was replaced by the Nursing and Midwifery Council (NMC) in April 2002.

4 In Chapter 3, we use the terminology 'issue-based' advocacy to refer to direct advocacy and 'systemic' advocacy to refer to public policy advocacy.

5 The National Occupational Standards for Social Work identify six key roles of a social worker. Key Role 3 states that social workers should support individuals to represent their needs, views and circumstances. An element of this role is to advocate with, and on behalf of, individuals, families, carers, groups and communities (Topps, England, 2003).

6 A school council is a school-based forum in which members are elected to represent the views of all children and young people in the school. They may include a number of school-based, student-led groups such as student forums and youth parliaments.

7 See Chapter 5.

8 See Chapter 6.

9 The Mental Capacity Act 2005 introduced a statutory right to an advocate and created the role of the Independent Mental Capacity Advocate relating to advocacy provision in England and Wales.

10 The Quality Protects (QP) Initiative was set up in 1998 to radically transform children's services in England. The programme initially had eight objectives (and additional sub-objectives) with a further three added in 1999. Objective 8 was 'to ensure that resources are planned and provided at levels which represent best value for money, allow for choice and different responses for different needs and circumstances', with Sub-objective 8.2 being to demonstrate: (a) that account is taken of the views of children and their families and (b) satisfaction by users with the services provided. Local authorities were therefore required to demonstrate that the views of children and their families were actively sought and used in the planning, delivery and review of services and to show increasing satisfaction with the services provided. In the Local Authority Circular LAC (99) 33, following the evaluation of the first round of the Quality Protects Management Action Plans, one of the priority areas for children's services was listening to the views and wishes of children, young people and their families. It stated that 'particular attention should be given to the involvement of young people collectively and to enhancing their individual voices through the development of independent advocacy services'.

11 The Children and Family Court Advisory and Support Service (CAFCASS) was established under the Criminal Justice and Courts Services Act 2000. It

brought together into one new service previously separate departments: the Family Court Welfare Service, the Children's branch of the Official Solicitor's Department and Local Authority Guardian ad litem and Reporting Officer Services. Guardians ad litem have been replaced by Children's Guardians, although their role remains that of 'an assessment of what is deemed to be in the best interests of the child'.

12   The Children Act 1989 requires local authorities to appoint an independent visitor for looked after children and young people who have had little or no contact with their parents for more than a year. Volunteers are expected to make friends with them, visiting regularly and helping them to participate in decisions about their future. However, the guidance is also clear that the independent visitor should not act as an advocate.

13   The appointment of an independent reviewing officer (IRO) is a legal requirement under Section 118 of the Adoption and Children Act 2002, which amended Section 26 of the Children Act 1989. The government issued the Review of Children's Cases (Amendment) (England) Regulations 2004 along with statutory guidance in September 2004. The regulations require all local authorities to have IROs in place to chair the statutory review meetings of all looked after children. The IROs are responsible for monitoring the local authority's review of the care plan, with the aim of ensuring that actions required to implement the care plan are carried out and outcomes monitored.

14   Independent reviewing officers are responsible for chairing decision-making meetings relating to the care of looked after children and young people.

15   For the general functions of Children's Commissioners, see the European Network of Commissioners website (www.ombudsnet.org).

16   Regulation 22 of the Children's Commissioner for Wales Regulations 2001.

17   See also the general functions of Commissioners (www.ombudsnet.org).

18   Article 6 of the Commissioner for Children and Young People (Northern Ireland) Order 2003 states this as a 'principal aim' of the Commissioner.

19   See Article 6 (iii)(b) of the Children and Young People (Northern Ireland) Order 2003.

20   For functions of the Commissioner, see Section 41 (i) of the Children and Young People (Scotland Act) 2003.

21   See section 52 (ii) of the Children and Young People (Scotland Act) 2003.

22   See Section 2 (3)(a–e) of the Children Act 2004.

23   For functions of the Commissioner, see Section 2 (1)(a–e) of the Children Act 2004.

# 2 Childhood, children's rights and advocacy

Human rights are general rights, rights that arise from no special undertaking beyond membership of the human race. To have human rights one does not have to be anything other than a human being. Neither does one have to do anything other than be born as a human being.

(Donnelly 2003: 10)

## Introduction

Independent advocacy services for children and young people have developed alongside understanding about the impact of 'adultism', which has the potential to silence the voices of children and young people. Adultism is a term that has been used to explain the oppression of children and young people by adults. For Barford and Wattam (1991), adultism is something that 'has the same power dimension as sexism and racism and it is such a pervasive phenomenon as to be almost unrecognisable and taken for granted' (p. 99). It has been suggested that during the 1990s children and young people as a group were systematically ignored and denied access to forums where they could be heard, making adultism a more oppressive material and intellectual force than ageism (Scraton 1997). This characterizes children and young people as a low-status group in relation to adults. The consequent marginalization of children and young people is evident in adult attitudes and behaviours that fail to recognize, for example, children's capacity to determine their own lives (Qvortrup 1994). In his analysis of social changes over the past thirty years, Parton (2006) suggests that while children and young people have been placed at the centre of policies and practices (recognizing that they are persons in their own right), concerns about safeguarding vulnerable children and young people has resulted in increasing control and regulation of their lives – which in turn regulates and constrains their agency.

The development of advocacy for children and young people has been influenced by discourses of childhood and children's rights. To understand adult attitudes to advocacy and the need for children and young people to have access to independent advocacy, it is therefore critical to examine literature about constructions of childhood. This cannot be understood in isolation from perspectives on children's rights, since these indicate how policy and practice have responded to changing views of childhood and attempted to legitimate a concept of advocacy. In this chapter, we will therefore begin by considering ways in which childhood is understood before going on to look at liberationist and protectionist perspectives on children's rights and a model for understanding rights based on an understanding of adult/child power relations. This will take us into a discussion about citizenship and consideration about the significance of the United Nations Convention on the Rights of the Child.

## Understanding childhood

> And sometimes when you ask adults for something they'll ask you all these questions and they know you're stuck and you can't say anything until you just give up.
>
> (Willow 2002: 33)

The way that children and young people are understood and treated needs to be located within the broader context of childhood. Childhood has been seen as a distinct stage of life in relation to adulthood during most of the twentieth century. However, thinking about childhood has changed over time, which has influenced adult attitudes and policy initiatives in relation to children and young people in health, education and social care. Literature reflects the construction of childhood as both problematic and contested, in which children and young people are set apart from adults (Archard 1993; Qvortrup 1994; Hill and Tisdall 1997; Lee 2001). Childhood is constructed by factors such as age, gender, ethnicity, ability, sexuality and social class. It is not a universal category and it does not have universal features, as experiences of childhood are inevitably shaped by family, environmental, economic and socio-political conditions (Hart 1997). Within a UK context, the experiences of children such as those excluded from school, children in prisons, young carers, children living in poverty, disabled children, unaccompanied children seeking asylum and children in the care system contribute to our understanding of the reality and complexity of contemporary childhood. Discussions about childhood therefore reflect the diverse contexts of children's lives, experiences and relationships. However, western views of childhood tend to promote a conception of childhood that reinforces dependency and domesticity (Thomas 2000), ignoring the experiences of, for example, street children or child soldiers.

Dominant models of childhood have also been criticized for being Eurocentric and paying insufficient attention to considerations of race and ethnicity (Graham 2007b; Robinson 2007). This has led to a 'deficit' approach in models of childhood, rather than a strengths approach that takes into account the diversity of children's experiences and the importance of race and culture in children's development. Contributions from black psychologists who have explored the intersection between African and African-American culture and the development of black children has led to a greater understanding of the relationship between, for example, culture and social cognition (Shade 1991).

The disciplines of psychology and sociology have been influential in developing understandings of childhood. From the 1940s, *psychological* theories began to build up a body of knowledge, which had a marked impact on both discourses of childhood and on education and social welfare policy and practice (Hill and Tisdall 1997). Divergent and at times misunderstood, they have nevertheless made a significant contribution to understanding about childhood as well as influencing, for example, controversial debates around areas such as physical punishment (Flekkoy 1988). Most psychological theories in relation to childhood are underpinned by the notion of human development. Developmental perspectives situate childhood as a stage in the life cycle, characterized by dependency and immaturity. Childhood is further subdivided through a series of distinct age spans and transitions. Stage-based models can be criticized for reinforcing the notion that children lack the capacity to be involved in decision making at certain stages (or ages) (Lansdown 1997). Nevertheless, children clearly begin their lives in a position of dependency on the caring decisions of adults (Hart 1997). They should then be assisted by the family and other institutions to become more able to act as their own agents, acknowledging that increasingly making their own decisions is an essential element of their development as adults. It has been suggested that the concept of 'evolving capacity' offers an alternative to ideas about competency that are based on age (Lansdown 2005).

Early *sociological* perspectives on childhood have also been criticized for portraying children as needing to develop or emerge as 'complete beings' (Thomas 2000; Lee 2001). At birth children are unaware of the societal norms and conventions of a particular culture. Through the process of socialization, however, they become informed about these social conventions, which become internalized – children are therefore effectively 'made social' (Thomas 2000: 15). Such thinking impacts on understanding about the validity of children's voices. Discussing the 'silencing' of children, Lee (2001) argues that traditional perspectives have consistently deprived children of their voices. He observes that central to the idea of the socialization of children is that 'before they can participate fully in social life, before they can say anything worth hearing, they need to be socialised. When children speak, they

necessarily speak out of ignorance of social convention' (p. 89). These traditional perspectives have reinforced the idea that children's voices are unreli-
able and the more dependent a child is, the less likely their views will
be elicited or taken seriously – here adult sources that take a 'best interests'
perspective on behalf of a child are seen as the reliable alternative.

Qvortrup (1990, 1994) has challenged the notion that childhood is simply
a stage on the way to achieving adulthood. He argues that children should not
be positioned as 'not yets' or 'becomings' but as beings. They are 'social actors'
who, either as individuals or collectively, have an impact on childhood and in
shaping it. Rather than being just a period in the life-course, childhood can
therefore be described as a structural feature of societies (Hendrick 2000). In
their seminal work exploring the construction of childhood, James and Prout
(1990) develop a paradigm that acknowledges that children are social actors
and that their experiences are 'worthy of social analysis'. What has been
described as the 'new' sociology of childhood challenges concepts of childhood as universal and the image of children as incomplete. Instead, children
and young people are seen as active participants rather than passive recipients
of social welfare provision. As 'social beings' in their own right, children's own
voices reflect the reality of their lives. The discourse of social construction has
also influenced thinking about the value of children's perspectives and secured
greater legitimacy for promoting children's participatory and citizenship
rights informed by children's accounts. Asserting that childhood is a social
rather than a biological construct, it re-frames childhood as a construct of
society at any given time constituted by social and historical features, and
recognizes the significance of varying theoretical understandings and cultural
representations (James and Prout 1990). Although this perspective is not without its critics (Lavalette and Cunningham 2002), it has been central in promoting debate about the status of children and young people in an adult world
and, therefore, raising awareness of the need for access to advocacy support to
enable their status as citizens to be fully recognized.

These debates about the construction of childhood are therefore important in considering the relationship between children's participation and the
role of advocacy. The 'new' sociology of childhood has had an impact on
perceptions of children and young people as social actors with their own perspective and ability to influence decision making. This has challenged more
traditional thinking about childhood, and has led to the development of participatory ways of working. However, the contribution of psychological perspectives is also relevant to the emergence of advocacy. For example, there is
often ambivalence about the involvement of younger children or disabled
children and young people in decision-making processes that concern their
lives. This is invariably based on age-based ideas about capacity, or in the case
of disabled children assumptions made about their impairment. While all theories of childhood recognize the evolving capacity of children and young

people, children are more likely to be denied participation rights on the basis of age. However, while children who are physically or mentally immature, have relatively little experience and lack knowledge are likely to be more vulnerable, this does not necessarily mean that they cannot have a view about what is happening in their lives and be given the opportunity to participate at some level (Lansdown 2005). Understanding discourses of childhood helps us to understand the contribution that advocacy can make to promoting children's and young people's participatory rights. The relationship between the *capacity* to participate and *opportunities* to participate is very relevant here. Lansdown argues that the capacity to participate can be learned if the opportunities are provided. In situations where parents, teachers, mentors or other key people in the lives of children may find it difficult to provide such opportunities, independent advocates may be well placed to provide them.

## Understanding transitions

The notion of transition in relation to work with children and young people has tended to be associated with the move from 'dependence' to 'relative independence'. However, a wider definition encompasses more broadly the diversity of situations children and young people may face within the complexity of their lives. A transition can therefore be seen as:

> any episode where children are having to cope with the potentially challenging episodes of change, including progressing from one developmental stage to another, changing schools, entering or leaving the care system, loss, bereavement, parental incapacity or entry to adulthood.
>
> (Newman and Blackburn 2002: 1)

Transitions can be understood in various ways. Some of the more commonly experienced and expected transitions include starting school, starting work and beginning to live independently. Transitions may also occur for some young people as a result of unexpected life experiences such as family breakdown, unemployment, redundancy, disability, serious illness or the death of a parent. Advocates are more likely to work with children and young people who are experiencing the following types of transition: entering or leaving the care system; being adopted; being excluded from school; entering or leaving prison (young people in young offenders' institutions); moving from children's services to adult services; or adapting to living in a different country (refugees and asylum seekers)

In Box 2.1 we can see that Tom's transition into the prison system was difficult, although it improved with the personal support of the officer and

---

**Box 2.1**   Case study: Tom

Tom (age 16) is a young white person whose experience of arriving at a young offenders' institution for the first time was that he was going into prison. He was already upset about receiving a prison sentence – which he had not expected – and felt lonely, frightened and worried about his mother. He was admitted with another young person, Angus (age 17), who had warned him to be strong and to watch out for bullies. When they arrived in reception, Angus and Tom were separated and placed in different wings, which increased Tom's anxiety. An officer found him sitting on his own and noted his distress – by this time Tom was talking about self-harming and the officer, recognizing how upset he was, tried to reassure Tom. The officer therefore opened an Assessment, Care in Custody and Teamwork (ACCT) document. After Tom had said that he felt that no-one was listening to him or understood what he was going through, the officer told Tom about the independent advocacy service and explained that all new admissions had the right to talk to an advocate within the first week.

Tom met with the advocate the following morning, by which time he was very anxious, upset and he felt he could not trust anyone to talk to in the prison. The advocate was able to support him to share his worries and fears. Tom was particularly keen to move to the same wing as Angus where he felt he would be safer. The advocate highlighted the need for Tom to talk to the staff so that they could be more aware of his feelings and could try to help him. She also told him about the role of the advocate and explained about the ACCT review process. Following this, the advocate met with the senior officer who instigated an ACCT review and Tom was soon moved to the other wing, which consequently lessened his anxiety and went some way to helping him to manage this difficult transition.

---

information about access to an independent advocate. This helped Tom to access and understand the care-planning system for prisoners[1].

It is useful to look briefly at some of the debates in this area, especially since the difficulties that some young people may face is becoming recognized in policy and legislation. For example:

- 'Valuing People: A New Strategy for Learning Disabilities for the 21st Century' emphasizes that transition planning needs to be person-centred: 'To help deliver the promise in the children's national service framework the person centred transition project has been introducing person centred approaches into the statutory transition planning process' (Department of Health 2001).
- The Special Education Needs (SEN) Code of Practice (DfES 2001a)

states that 'the views of young people themselves must be sought and recorded wherever possible in any assessment, reassessment or review during the years of transition. Personal advisors, student counsellors, advocates or advisors, teachers and other school staff, social workers or peer support may be needed to support the young person in the transition process'.

- Section 10 of the SEN toolkit specifically addresses transition planning for students who are statemented and clearly indicates the involvement of advocates: 'Schools should also have information on local sources of help and advice, including . . . and offer independent advice and advocacy if required' (DfES 2001b). The toolkit also recognizes the importance of encouraging children's and young people's self-advocacy skills to improve their participation.
- National Standards for Leaving Care recognize the importance of ensuring that young people from care are able to make a successful transition into adult life (www.leavingcare.org). The Children (Leaving Care) Act 2000 provides for pathway plans to facilitate the transition from care to independence.

There are therefore some young people for whom policy and practice have identified that transitions are particularly difficult and who may need advocacy support to help them manage this point in their lives. Research with young learning disabled people has identified that the transition from children to adult services is often both problematic and badly managed. This is highlighted in 'Valuing People' (Department of Health 2001), which indicates that young people tend not to be involved in the decision making about their lives and that there is a lack of coordination between services, which can lead to their exclusion from adult services. Consequently, the Special Educational Needs Toolkit (DfES 2001b) sets out what should be included in a transition plan for young people who have been statemented. Similarly, young people using child and adolescent mental health services and young people with long-term health conditions may find the transfer to adult services difficult and the need for young people using these services to have access to advocacy support has been identified in guidance (Department of Health 2006a, 2008).

Care leavers are also likely to find the transition to independence hard. This is recognised in the Children (Leaving Care) Act 2000, which amended the provisions of the Children Act 1989 in relation to young people leaving care. The Act imposes a new duty on local authorities 'to meet the needs of eligible 16–17 year olds in care (eligible children) or care leavers (relevant children), those who were eligible or relevant before reaching 18 (former relevant children)' (Brammer 2007: 321). At 16 each young person must have a written pathway plan that maps out their route to independence.

Finally, young carers may find the transition to adulthood a complex process. For example, Dearden and Becker's (2000) research examining young carers' transitions into adulthood drew attention to the impact of caring on young people's lives. They concluded that some young people had 'inappropriate caring responsibilities' that shaped choices such as when to leave home and decisions about education and training – a time when advocacy support might be needed. This is exacerbated by the fact that many education, health and social work professionals do not appear to have sufficient understanding of the circumstances of young carers and the challenges faced by the estimated 175,000 young carers in the UK. Young carers are often unaware therefore of their rights to an assessment of their needs or the support they are entitled to[2] (Underdown 2002).

We can see that that involving children and young people in shaping their future is an important element of the transition to adulthood. The study of transitions, which considers the way in which social, legal and political institutions structure the process of growing up, is therefore helpful in understanding the need for advocacy support.

## Perspectives on rights

It has been pointed out that attitudes to children's rights fundamentally reflect the values and prejudices of society at particular points in time (Jenkins 2003). Presenting children and young people both as less powerful and less competent than adults and therefore needing protection, as well as oppressed and therefore needing increased opportunities for autonomy and self-determination (Hart 1997), feeds varying perspectives and debates that have been put forward concerning children's rights based on notions of the adult/child relationship. Lindsay (1992) identifies three broad perspectives on rights: liberationist, protectionist and pragmatist, which provide a useful starting point when analysing debates about and responses to children's and young people's rights. In addition, they provide insight into the complex relationships between young people, their families and social welfare practitioners, who may hold varied positions on what can be seen as a rights continuum.

*Liberationists* have been associated with the work of liberal campaigners and philanthropists who sought better treatment and conditions for children[3], as well as more controversial writers such as Holt (1975) and Farson (1978). However, the liberationist perspective emerged much earlier from educationalists. The radical educationalist A.S. Neill, who founded Summerhill School, was himself influenced in the early twentieth century by an American based in Britain, Homer Lane. Neill challenged perceptions of how children should be educated, believing that children and adults should have equal rights both in the private sphere of the home and the public space. John Holt (1975) was a key representative of the liberationist perspective. Holt (1975: 210) argued in *Escape from Childhood: The Needs and Rights of Children* that being a child meant 'being wholly subservient and dependent'. Both Holt and Farson promoted children's rights to self-determination and autonomy. They asserted that children should have the right to work, vote, have financial independence, be able to choose where and with whom they live, and have sexual freedom. They promoted the view that children should be treated in the same way as adults, arguing that the state should not distinguish between citizens on the grounds of age or maturity with access to the same rights adults – which means that neither the state nor parents should have special rights and powers over children and young people. In essence, age distinctions should be removed. In so doing, not only did they make rights claims for children, but they also challenged society to justify the denial of children's rights (Wald 1979, cited in Thomas 2000).

The liberationist perspective is controversial, with commentators such as Fox-Harding (1996) arguing that liberationists do not fully explore the implications of full citizenship rights and responsibilities. This perspective is also challenged on the grounds that the evolving capacity of children indicates a need for protection as appropriate (Freeman 1983; Thomas 2000; Lansdown 2005). This is based on the premise that when children are young there is a responsibility on adults to enable them to develop knowledge and understanding as they mature. Such perspectives mirror the notion of childhood as a transition stage. However, Freeman (1983) also acknowledges that such a protectionist stance can also deny children the opportunity for the experiences they need to develop.

The *protectionist* approach has its origins in the 'child-saving' philosophies of the nineteenth century. The face of child labour was changed by the Industrial Revolution and led to the development of philanthropic organizations for whom children and young people became objects of concern. Legislation such as the 1908 Children Act introduced state education as a way of challenging the use of children and young people in the labour market. Such legislation was not received well by those who saw such legislation and the limits placed on child labour as contrary to the rights of fathers to bring up their children as they thought best (Pinchbeck and Hewitt 1969). However, attitudes to the traditional patriarchal family were also changing. The establishment of the National Society for the Prevention of Cruelty to Children (NSPCC) in 1889, and its subsequent campaign for legislation to protect children, led to legislation in 1889 to outlaw cruelty to children and to protect children in their own home. The work of the NSPCC was significant in promoting a protectionist perspective that had an impact on the subsequent development of child protection legislation and practice (Ferguson 2004) and on concepts of childhood (Hendrick 2003). Subsequent legislation and the high levels of state intervention in the lives of children and families has effectively been dominated by protectionist ways of thinking in the UK and Europe, and some of the rights encompassed by the UNCRC are also underpinned by protectionist principles. Within this perspective, adults are clearly seen as protectors of children's rights, but the approach also tends to view children and young people very much as objects of concern (Butler-Sloss 1988). It is beyond the remit of this book to chart the history of child protection. However, in terms of thinking about the development of advocacy, it could be argued that the dominance of the protectionist perspective has been a source of disempowerment of children and their families and consequently much of what advocates find that they need to counteract.

The difficult relationship between the privacy of the family and the responsibility of the state to protect vulnerable children and young people is epitomized in resistance to state intervention into family life (Goldstein et al. 1980). Goldstein and colleagues argued that intervention into family life should be the minimum necessary to safeguard the best interests of the child. Policy and legislation in the final decade of the last century has certainly tried to strike a balance between respecting the privacy of the family and protecting children – with legislation in the last two decades promoting partnership working with children and families. In tracing policy imperatives to safeguard childhood, however, Parton (2006) suggests that the development of integrated approaches to prevention has resulted in a number of policy initiatives focusing on early interventions and effectively widening policies 'designed for the few' so that they are 'seen as having relevance for the many' (p. 166). As such, Parton argues, children and young people are an increasingly regulated and surveyed group, whose lives are measured by targets and outcomes: such regulation is unlikely to support the voice and agency of children and young people.

Furthermore, children and young people in western cultures are not allowed to make mistakes and learn from them, nor are they encouraged to express their own views gradually over a period of time (Freeman 2000), which would support and promote their confidence and enhance their capacity to be involved in and make decisions for themselves. It is interesting to note that in countries like Nicaragua, where the assessment and management of risk is part of the daily lives of children and young people, the approach taken by a participation worker would be to encourage and strengthen their considerable skills in this area. In contrast, rather than educate and empower children and young people to understand and assess risk to identify ways of protecting themselves (both individually and collectively), professional child care practitioners and parents in the UK – fearful of the consequences of failing in their responsibilities – are more likely to prevent them from encountering any risk (Shier 2009).

It has also been suggested that it is possible to hold simultaneously a liberationist and protectionist position, as the differences between adults and children are not only founded on differential power positions, but relate to various thresholds of competence (Franklin 1986, 1995). This *pragmatic* approach recognizes that children need the opportunity to express their own views within the context of their evolving capacity – progressively taking on more decisions for themselves (Lindsay 1992). Pragmatists are regarded by Lindsay as also supporting children's rights. However, the defining feature of this approach is promotion of the rights of children and young people within legislative structures and policies that are defined and imposed by adults. This then means that rights to participation have to be balanced by regard to their best interests (Hill and Tisdall 1997).

Lindsay (1992) argues that the foundation of the pragmatic approach is based on the work of various organizations fighting for the rights of children and young people. He cites advocacy organizations among these groups. Lindsay bases his analysis on the fact that campaigns of early advocacy organizations focused on the statutory right to have access to complaints procedures – that is, they were working within established structures. Certainly it is hard to challenge this view since advocacy organizations have subsequently fought for the mandatory right to an advocate in supporting children and young people to make a complaint, and the provision of advocacy services are often focused on finding ways to enable young people to come to voice within adult mechanisms.

Effectively, we can see that children's and young people's rights can be understood along a continuum, with liberationist approaches at one end, protectionist at the other and pragmatists in the middle. Some pragmatic approaches lean towards the liberationist perspective, while for others their pragmatism will have more of a protectionist stance. We believe that the early development of child and youth advocacy was strongly influenced by the liberationist end of the continuum. However, more recently, with government intervention in the provision of advocacy and criticisms that liberationists fail to recognize both that children need protection and have acknowledged developmental needs, it is persuasive and possibly more comfortable for advocates to hold a pragmatic position to children's rights. We believe that this is worrying and raises a number of issues for advocacy. Primarily there is a need for independent advocacy to maintain a radical edge. Child care professionals rightly have to work from a rights perspective underpinned by a best interests approach. However, there is an imperative here for independent advocates to be very clear that their perspective will be more informed by the liberationist end of the continuum. If we think about this in terms of issues of confidentiality, we can see that the exception to the confidentiality principle of the National Standards for the Provision of Children's Advocacy Services is obviously informed by protectionist perspectives. Standard 7 (7.3) states that 'nothing will be disclosed outside the service without their agreement unless it is necessary to prevent significant harm to them or to someone else, or if disclosure is required by a court order' (Department of Health 2002; Welsh Assembly Government 2003).

Waterhouse (2003) expressed deep concerns in this respect when the Standards were first published. Based on his experiences of hearing evidence from young people who had been abused in the looked after system in North Wales, he makes a compelling case. He argues that although children and young people made initial complaints about their abuse in the care system, the subsequent process resulted in very few pursuing them. This involved a senior member of staff seeing a child or young person about their complaint to ascertain whether they wanted to make a formal complaint and 'warning' them about the consequences to the abuser and to the child concerned. In this respect, protectionist principles constrain the independence of advocates, which in turn may make it difficult for them to develop a meaningful relationship with children and young people. Waterhouse highlights the very real tensions that exist between protectionist and liberationist perspectives in relation to advocacy and safeguarding children and young people:

> my fear to the intended exception to the confidentiality principle and the warning to be given about it to the child is that it will stifle the potential relationship between advocate and child in many cases at the onset and reinforce suspicion that the advocate is merely another agent of the 'authority' . . . if the advocate/child relationship is to work, however, very full weight must be given to the confidentiality principle as is it in law. Any exception to it should be defined very narrowly and clearly and I do not regard the present phraseology as satisfactory.
>
> (Waterhouse 2003: 22)

The radical edge of advocacy may also be eroded through the commissioning of independent advocacy services. The promotion of children's rights has the support of governments, commissioners of services and advocacy organizations. However, clearly different stakeholders will be on different points of the rights continuum, which will influence the type of advocacy service they commission and the level of autonomy they allow a service. The current climate of advocacy through service level agreements means that there is a danger that advocacy services could be more informed by protectionist approaches to children's rights than liberationist values. Advocacy services are provided for commissioning agencies that target advocacy services for particular children and young people, which means that access to advocacy can be limited and controlled by the criteria of funders. Commissioners also have the ability to terminate funding contracts for advocacy. Since research has shown that relationships between health and social care professionals and advocates can sometimes be difficult (Oliver 2008), there is the possibility that uncertainty about future funding may constrain advocates' ability to enable children and young people to gain more control over their own lives.

This highlights the contradictions at the heart of contemporary advocacy, which means that advocates either work on behalf of children and young people, consequently failing to challenge their dependent position in society – passive advocacy; or they challenge the status of children and young people by encouraging and supporting them to actively take their own action – active advocacy (Jenkins 1995). Advocates who are commissioned to work within existing systems, such as complaints procedures, child protection, looked after children's reviews, young offenders' adjudication and planning meetings, mental health tribunals or education transitions planning meetings, may be more likely to engage in passive forms of advocacy, with the consequent main-tenance of the status quo. Often children and young people find these systems difficult and choose either not to attend or to attend but preferring the advo-cate to speak for them. Effectively, then, they are working within existing adult-led systems and failing to challenge the nature of (protectionist) decision making as well as challenging the position of children and young people within society.

In Box 2.2, overleaf, the advocacy experienced by Matty enabled him to take action to change his circumstances, which in turn also challenged the attitudes and assumptions of the professionals in the meeting towards him. Here, Matty's advocate supported him to take action, through writing what he wanted the Conference to hear, to make his life better. Matty was encouraged as far as possible to actively take his own action. Arguably as the advocate was still working within the statutory framework, there was an element of passive advocacy here. However, in many ways the role the advocate tried to take in this instance was to work with Matty towards breaking down the barriers that serve to reinforce the position of the adult professionals, to enable him to come to voice. This points to the need for independent advocates, as critical practitioners, to locate advocacy within the wider context of practice and understand the power relations that exist in any given situation. This then facilitates resistance to the protectionist end of the continuum and more active approaches to advocacy practice.

## A framework of rights

We have seen in the previous section that 'working from a rights-based per-spective' is complex. There is no straightforward concept of children's rights and the construction of childhood as understood in the UK and western cultures is relatively recent. It is not easy to balance what appear to be the competing imperatives of rights, the best interest approach and liberationist perspectives. Raising an awareness of the role of and need for advocacy

---

**Box 2.2**  Case study: Matty

---

Matty attended part of his Child Protection Conference and asked his advocate to present his contribution:

*This is what I want to say: I don't remember some things the report said happened. I can't remember what my Mum was like last year as I was too worried about what would happen to me. It was good when Stacie [his half sister] came back – it is good when someone else is here when my Mum has been drinking. I am sad now Stacie has gone again – I miss her 'cos I could talk to her and she did nice things with me like swimming. I still want to live with my Mum.*

*I know when Mum has been drinking. She sounds funny. She is cheerful when she is drunk but not all of the time and she also gets mad and angry and loud and then tired. I don't know what would help her to stop. When she drinks she lies on the sofa and I put a quilt on her and put her head on the pillow. I make a cup of coffee for her in the morning and make myself a sandwich. I quite often feel upset and I don't know why. I used to go swimming but haven't been able to go for ages. We don't have much money. I wish that I could earn some to help out.*

Matty's contribution gave the professionals involved insight into his resilience and his vulnerability. He indicated the things that he felt needed to be included in a plan to improve his situation. This was the starting point of his contribution to the assessment process. He identified that he needed:

- to have someone else in the house to share the difficult times;
- to have good quality information about plans being made for him;
- to be able to sort out some of his sad feelings;
- to have some activities to enjoy and to go swimming;
- to be able to earn some money;
- his role as a young carer to be identified.

(Adapted from Dalrymple and Horan 2008b)

---

involves child care practitioners and advocates not only understanding their personal position in respect of these perspectives but also understanding how to balance the different perspectives. Several theorists have suggested various typologies to make sense of varying views on children's rights. We have found the most helpful of these to be a model by Jenkins (2003), which moves beyond thinking about rights as abstract concepts or idealistic notions of entitlement or expectation to understanding rights in terms of power. He draws on Freeman's (1983) categorization of rights:

- welfare rights and human rights
- protection
- social justice
- choice and autonomy

*β participation*

Jenkins develops Freeman's work in a framework that is based on under-standing the power relations that exist between children and adults at any given moment and the ability of children and young people to act independ-ently of adults. His analysis therefore emphasizes the relational nature of power *vis-à-vis* adults and young people at a particular instant. Adults have the power to deny children and young people rights and this is likely to happen when children and young people are viewed by adults as their prop-erty or possessions. However, the balance of power changes when children are seen as more autonomous in their own right, which equates to notions of active citizenship. Their rights to take action independently of adults are then recognized and respected. In between these two positions, however, children and young people may be seen as needing protection – where the power of the adult is not to deny rights but is used to make and enforce decisions without their involvement in the process. Where power is shared through involve-ment in decision making, children and young people become participants in the decision-making processes rather than objects needing protection. The model offers a way to bring together both liberationist and protectionist per-spectives into a framework that enables us to translate these theories into practice. It can help advocates and child care practitioners to make sense of the complex power relations that exist when working with children and families.

We can see from the model (Box 2.3) that practitioners can be operating within a rights perspective at different points on the continuum. Within the context of multi-disciplinary working, it is likely that practitioners will encounter policies, procedures and practices that reflect various aspects of the continuum. For example, the UNCRC can be said to embody negative rights in that they are framed as rights not to be mistreated or abused. Negative rights equate with the protectionist perspective epitomized in type 2 rights in the model. Participation rights can be described as neutral rights as set out in the Children Act 1989 and the third typology of Jenkins model. Finally, positive rights are those of active citizenship and represent the liberationist end of the continuum.

One of the problems with this model is that it does not address structural issues. To some extent, it underplays the complexities of children's and young people's lives and the impact of institutional power. It reinforces a dichotom-ous position between adults and children and young people that places them as binary opposites. Although the model allows for movement, it also locates adults and children in terms that do not recognize the interdependency of

| Box 2.3 | Jenkins' model of children's rights | | | |
|---|---|---|---|---|
| | *Power of adult* | | *Power of child* | |
| *Type of rights* | *1* | *2* | *3* | *4* |
| *Child's role in relation to adults* | Child or young person holds no rights independent of parents or adults | Child or young person has rights to welfare and protection that are decided and enforced by adults | Child or young person has the right to be consulted about decision made for him or her | Child or young person has the right to choose and to take action independently of parents or adults |
| *Child's perceived status* | Child is seen as the property or possession of adults | Child is seen as an object needing protection by adults: Negative rights | Child is seen as a participant in adult decision-making processes: Neutral rights | Child is seen as an active citizen: Positive rights |
| *Example* | Parents have the right to remove children from sex education classes. The legislation makes no reference to seeking or taking account of children's views and opinions in this respect | Children have the right not to be denied an education (set out in the European Convention on Human Rights) | Before making a decision about a child or young person in child care proceedings, their wishes and feelings have to be placed before that court and taken into account (Children Act 1989) | A child has the right of access to most computerized or handwritten records held on him or her |
| | | | | (Adapted from Jenkins 2003) |

adult/child relations or value difference. In effect, there is an implication here that children and young people are devalued in relation to adults and that their powerless positions are fixed or immutable.

## Children and citizenship

Two dominant and polarized ways of conceptualizing children are evident in debates about childhood and children's rights (Roche 1999b), in which children are either portrayed as in need of protection (from themselves or others; i.e. 'child as victim') or as dangerous and in need of discipline (i.e. 'child as threat') (Daniel and Ivatts 1998). For Jenks (1996), both concepts have been dominant throughout the twentieth century and have informed debates about care and control in social welfare policy, legislation and practice, and children's rights discourses. More recent conceptualizations include children as citizens and children as investment (DfES 2005; Hendrick 2005).

Citizenship as a concept has the potential for development to provide rights for *all* groups of people including young people. However, it is a contested concept with a range of definitions. T.H. Marshall's (1950) conceptualization of citizenship provides the building blocks used in other conceptualizations (Lister 2008). He offers a framework of collective rights that seek to provide respect, freedom and equality of status for the individual. There are three principal components:

- Civil – individual freedom of speech, thought and liberty, maintained through the judicial system.
- Political – the right to access the political system.
- Social – the right to basic economic welfare, social security and living standards, administered though employment or public institutions.

While this classic definition of citizenship has endured, and is dominant within youth and social policy (Jeffs 2005), there are limitations to Marshall's analysis. Citizenship can be seen as a mechanism for exclusion as well as inclusion. Traditional views of citizenship can therefore be seen as unequal, with different social groups experiencing difference or inequality in terms of rights. Coles (1995) points out that Marshall's view ignores the position of other members of society: women, disabled people, black and minority ethnic groups and, significantly, children and young people. Social class is not examined, which would identify the structural inequality within the family and the wider community that children and young people experience. This is evident in the range of civil, political and social rights that come to young people as they age, for example rights to have a tattoo, have a 'paper round', drive, have sex, vote, marry or receive benefits. Feminists also have been critical of general conceptualizations of citizenship that are inherently gendered. Women's initial exclusion from citizenship was premised on their dependency and perceived lack of competence and rationality. Such reasons are similarly used to deny citizenship to children and young people. Lansdown (1995) observes that children's exclusion from citizenship is also underpinned by the protectionist discourses discussed earlier in this chapter with an emphasis on age and understanding rather than children's capacity.

Citizenship for children and young people essentially means inclusion as legitimate members of society whose voices and perspectives are valued (Willow and Neale 2004). There are clear links here between membership of society and children's participation. Roche (1999b) draws on Minow's (1987) analysis, indicating that children's participation in a community recasts their status from exclusion to membership. Examining the language of citizenship in his consideration of the position of children in society Roche (1999a) suggests that participation and the language of rights embodied within the UNCRC encourages their agency and implies a more active role for children and young people. He goes on to suggest the need to rethink citizenship and reconsider the language of rights to include children and young people. Roche encourages us to move beyond thinking about the acquisition of voice to an inclusive politics for young people, which is aware of the context in which participation is offered. He links the need for advocacy to this process, observing that:

> The languages of participation and empowerment are cosy but we need to be more critical of the circumstances of inclusion and the kinds of adult support (e.g. advocacy and representation) that children might need. In this sense the children's rights projects and emerging demands for 'inclusion' as citizens involves a redrawing of what it is to be an adult and a child'.
>
> (Roche 1999: 489)

## The United Nations Convention on the Rights of the Child

The children's rights movement has had a significant impact on the development of advocacy services, partly because rights and the related concept of citizenship constitute a powerful modern discourse (Hill and Tisdall 1997; Boylan and Ing 2005). Recognition of children's rights, consolidated by the UNCRC, has led to widespread acknowledgement of the principles of the Convention in the provision of care and services for children and young people, and has given impetus to debates about children's citizenship and rights status: 'Overall, the coverage and scope of the UNCRC in recognising the rights of children and young people, and setting out how they are to be both promoted and protected is unrivalled in terms of their comprehensive nature' (Kilkelly and Lundy 2006: 333).

The UNCRC was ratified by the UK in 1991 and sets out internationally agreed minimum standards for children and young people under the age of eighteen. The 54 articles contained in the Convention include two that underpin the principles of advocacy, children's rights to freedom of expression and to be listened to. More broadly, the articles cover key aspects of children's and young people's lives, including: non-discrimination, protection, play, liberty, family life, health and information support, having decisions made in their best interests, awareness of the UNCRC and education.

In ratifying the Convention, governments agree to comply with the Convention's provisions and are required to report back to the UN Committee on the Rights of the Child, initially after two years and thereafter every five years, detailing progress made in implementing the Convention. Importantly, in assessing the report, the United Nations Committee also considers reports from non-governmental organizations (NGOs). For example, The Children's Rights Development Unit (CRDU) was set up in 1992 to encourage implementation of the Convention across the UK. It published the *UK Agenda for Children* in 1994, which analysed how far law policy and practice in the UK complied with the Convention's standards and submitted a report to the UN Committee. The *UK Agenda for Children* was committed to ensuring that children and young people informed the report and worked closely with Article 12[4], a children's rights organization led by young people (Children's Rights Development Unit 1994). The UK Government's first and subsequent reports to the UN Committee have been criticized for shortcomings in its commitment to the implementation of the UNCRC. Reports from NGOs include those from children and young people following national consultations. For example, Article 12 (Scotland) submitted an alternative report to the UN Committee in 2008, *I Witness UNCRC in Scotland*, which made a number of recommendations, including an interesting observation about participation and the use of adult-instigated participatory structures such as youth parliaments, youth fora and student councils. They state that such structures fail to meet the needs of the majority of children and young people in Scotland and question their democratic legitimacy, since the small group is unlikely to represent the wider population. Such arguments can also be applied to collective advocacy groups and to those children and young people who sit on management committees of independent advocacy services in all four nations of the UK (Cairns 2006).

The philosophy that underpins advocacy is the belief that children and young people have a fundamental right to a voice in the decision-making processes that impact on their lives and should also be recognized as citizens. These ideas have developed as a result of major milestones reached by those advocating children's civil, social, cultural and political rights: notably the

1924 Geneva Declaration on the Rights of the Child; the 1949 United Nations Declaration of Human Rights; and the 1989 United Nations Declaration on the Rights of the Child. Such human rights instruments have sought to assure social, cultural, economic and political rights (Flekkoy and Kaufman 1997; Boylan and Braye 2006). Emphasis has centred on the balance between children's participatory and protective rights. This is evident in the connectedness of articles within the UNCRC to ensure the survival, protection, development and participation of children and young people. The Convention also recognizes that children need care and protection because of their vulnerability and need support to be able to enjoy their rights. To balance these two aspects, Article 3 of the Convention states that it is the best interests of the child that must be the primary consideration in any actions relating to them and not the interests of parents, carers or the state. Linked to this is a second principle, seen in Article 12, which asserts that the views of the child are to be heard, respected and taken seriously in all matters affecting them. However, the participatory provision of Article 12 (i) and (ii) does conceptualize participation subject to the child's age and maturity. Article 12 and related provisions of Articles 13–16 reflect the spirit of participation and incorporate an interpretation of rights to which children and young people are entitled. However, Article 12 does not ensure that a child's or young person's views will be adhered to. Within the English judicial system, courts have tended to regard the ultimate decision as resting with the courts. The caveat 'due weight' is sufficient to allow scope for judicial, professional and parental discretion. Implementation is therefore usually a matter for domestic interpretation. For an illustrative example, see the wording of the welfare checklist contained in Section 1 (3)(a) Children Act 1989 regarding children's wishes and feelings.

The series of 'participation articles' in the UNCRC, described as 'visionary articles which recognised children as developing citizens' (Hart 1997:11), have led to arguments for denying children participation rights, based on concerns about lack of competency and the wisdom of experience (Franklin 2002; 1995). However participation projects have demonstrated that, given the opportunity, children and young people have the capacity to be competent active citizens (Cutler 2002; Willow 2002). Recognizing that many nations are having to consider how to balance children's needs for protection with their participatory rights, Hart (1997) points out that the UNCRC can be useful as 'an instrument of persuasion for those persons wishing to promote the idea of children as independent, thinking subjects capable and deserving of a greater degree of participation' (p. 11). Its impact, therefore, is significant in considering how children and young people should be perceived and treated, and underpins recognition of the need for them to have advocacy support to ensure their participatory rights. Kilkelly and Lundy (2006) found that the Convention contains language that can be used meaningfully within an audit process, as within Article 12: 'its unequivocal language and strongly inferred

---

**Box 2.4** Articles of the UNCRC adopted by the General Assembly of the United Nations 1989

---

*Article 3 (i)*
In all actions concerning the child, whether undertaken by public or private social welfare institutions, courts of law, administrative authorities or legislative bodies, the best interests of the child shall be a primary consideration

*Article 12 (ii)*
States Parties shall assure the child who is capable of forming his or her own views the right to express those views freely in all matters affecting the child, the views of the child being given due weight in accordance with the age and maturity of the child.

(2) For this purpose, the child shall in particular be provided with the opportunity to be heard in any judicial and administrative proceedings affecting the child, either directly, or through a representative or an appropriate body, in a manner consistent with the procedural rules of national law.

*Article 13 (ii)*
The child shall have the right to freedom of expression: this right shall include freedom to seek, receive and impart information and ideas of all kinds, regardless of frontiers, either orally, in writing or in print, in the form of art, or through any other media of the child's choice.

*Article 14 (i)*
States Parties shall respect the right of the child to freedom of thought, conscience and religion.

*Article 14 (ii)*
States Parties shall respect the rights and duties of the parents and, when applicable, legal guardians, to provide direction to the child in the exercise of his or her right in a manner consistent with the evolving capacities of the child.

*Article 15 (i)*
States Parties shall recognize the rights of the child to freedom of association and to freedom of peaceful assembly.

*Article 16 (i)*
No child shall be subjected to arbitrary or unlawful interference with his or her privacy, family, home or correspondence, nor to unlawful attacks on his or her honour or reputation

---

Continued

---

**Box 2.4** Continued

---

*Article 23 (i)*
States Parties shall recognize that a mentally or physically disabled child should enjoy a full and decent life, in conditions which ensure dignity, promote self-reliance, and facilitate the child's active participation in the community.

*Article 23 (iii)*
Recognizing the special needs of a disabled child, assistance extended in accordance with paragraph 2 of the present article shall be provided free of charge, whenever possible, taking into account the financial resources of parents or others caring for the child, and shall be designed to ensure that the disabled child has effective access to and receives education, training, health care services, rehabilitation services, preparation for employment and recreation opportunities in a manner conducive to the child's achieving the fullest possible social integration and individual development, including his or her cultural and spiritual development.

*Article 37*
. . . no child shall be deprived of his or her liberty unlawfully or arbitrarily. The arrest, detention or imprisonment of a child shall be in conformity with the law and shall only be used as a measure of last resort and for the shortest possible time. Every child deprived of liberty shall be treated with humanity and respect for the inherent dignity of the human person, and in a manner which takes into account the needs of persons of his or her age. In particular, every child deprived of liberty shall be separated from adults unless it is considered in the child's best interests not to do so . . .

*Article 40 (i)*
States Parties recognize the right of every child alleged as, accused of, or recognised as having infringed the penal law to be treated in a manner consistent with the promotion of the child's sense of dignity and worth which reinforces the child's respect for the human rights and fundamental freedoms of others . . .

*Article 42 (i)*
States parties undertake to make the principles and provisions of the Convention widely known, by appropriate and active means, to adults and children alike.

---

equation with the right to participation made it an effective benchmark against which law, policy and practice could be measured' (Kilkelly and Lundy 2006: 335). However, in attempting to use the UNCRC as an audit tool in their assessment of how far children's rights have been taken seriously in Northern

Ireland, they argue that some of the UNCRC's standards are inadequate. They also found it problematic transferring the UNCRC into measurable standards.

Inevitably, there are shortcomings in the Convention. For advocates, one of the most pertinent issues is the tension between Article 3, the best interests standard, and Article 12, the right to be heard. This is compounded by the fact that the concept of best interests lacks clarity and is not defined in any part of the Convention. Those drafting the Convention did not appear to view children and young people as active citizens, although they did see them as individuals with independent rights. The standards are guided by the protectionist end of the rights continuum, which recognizes that their rights need to be protected by parents and the state (Stahl 2007). This resonates with Franklin's observations about the way in which the rights of children and young people to protection are less controversial than their rights to participation and citizenship. Participatory rights challenge adults, as they have the potential to erode the idea of children belonging to their parents or, following Jenkins' (2003) model, the notion of children as 'possessions'. Therefore, participation can be seen by some as creating a divide between adults and children and young people (Lee 2005).

Education is another contentious area in relation to rights, especially for children and young people in the UK; indeed, two reports by the UN Committee on the Rights of the Child have been critical of the UK in terms of the participatory rights of children in education (Sherlock 2007)[5]. Children repeatedly raised the issue of lack of a voice in school decision-making processes in Kilkelly and Lundy's (2006) research. This is reflected in the alternative report to the UN Committee by Article 12 (Scotland), in which one of the recommendations included the proposal that the UNCRC should be included in teacher training curricula to facilitate the promotion of children's rights in schools. A third area of difficulty can be identified with regard to the provisions for disabled children and young people, where the emphasis of the Convention is on non-discrimination rather than inclusion (Freeman 2002). Kilkelly and Lundy are especially critical, describing Article 23 as 'grossly inadequate' in providing for disabled children's right to education, including special education needs and specialized health care. From this brief discussion of some of the challenges the Convention presents, we can see that while it underpins advocacy practice, there is also a role for advocates to be aware of the problems within the UNCRC in order to challenge areas where the rights of children and young people need to be strengthened.

Although the Children Act 1989 is positive with respect to the participation rights articulated in Article 12 (i) and (ii) of the UNCRC in the arena of public welfare, it is less so in private law, and in fact there are a number of disparities between the Convention and UK legislation (Freeman 2002). Recognizing that children and young people have a right to participate in decisions affecting their lives cuts across traditional notions of the power of parents/carers to exercise total control (Lansdown 1995). Their choices are constrained in 'their best interests', which can then become a rational for marginalizing children and young people for the convenience of adults (Hill and Tisdall 1997; Stahl 2007). One of the most common issues raised by children in Kilkelly and Lundy's (2006) research was related to this issue – they spoke about their desire for greater involvement in decision making within the family in relation to disputes with parents, lack of privacy in the home and problems with siblings. However, in Scotland the Children (Scotland) Act 1995 does impose on parents a duty to consult with children about major decisions that will affect their lives. For Roche (2002) such acknowledgement of the rights of children and young people within the family can be seen both as part of the democratization of family life and symbolically raises the status of the child or young person as a citizen.

## Summary

We have seen in this chapter that advocacy for children and young people has become established against a background of competing discourses in relation to the welfare of children and young people. These are encapsulated in both the protectionist/liberationist debates and in the nature of the right of children and young people to be active citizens. The discourses of childhood and rights inform the theory and practice of advocacy for children and young people and have a significant impact on how it is constructed. In broadly identifying the key elements of each concept we have explored how they interrelate. The debates indicate how attitudes towards children and young people are complex and sometimes contradictory. Traditionally, children and young people in western cultures have not always been encouraged to make reasoned and informed decisions about their lives, nor have they been invited to inform service delivery and planning. Rather, they have been regarded as objects of concern, passive recipients of a range of social, education and health interventions. However, attempts to challenge and question these assumptions have increasingly been made by protagonists across the children's rights spectrum. The tensions inherent in protectionist and liberationist perspectives on rights are reflected in policy, national legislation and international instruments. Nevertheless, the UNCRC is influential as a statement of moral principle and as a lobbying tool, although it is not part of domestic law in the UK and thus not directly enforceable. This differs from the Human Rights Act 1998, which in Section 19 requires an assessment of the compatibility of UK legislation with the provisions of the Act. In Wales, however, the Welsh Assembly Government has recognized the benefits of the UNCRC by formally adopting it as the basis for all their policy relating to children and young people. The National Standards for the Provision of Children's Advocacy

Services also clearly state that they are informed by Article 12 of the UNCRC, which they consider recognizes the changing views of children and childhood that they 'are not merely "adults in training" but people who are able to form and express opinions, to participate in decision-making processes and to influence solutions' (Department of Health 2002: 3; Welsh Assembly Government 2003: 3).

## Notes

1   Since April 2007, the Prison Service has used a care-planning system called Assessment, Care in Custody and Teamwork (ACCT) to help identify and care for prisoners at risk of suicide or self-harm. It aims to provide multidisciplinary support to prisoners in this situation. Young prisoners should be fully involved in the process.

2   Under the Carers and Disabled Children Act 2002, carers over the age of 16 are entitled to an assessment of their needs. It also authorizes the local authority to make direct payments to carers instead of providing services.

3   Successful campaigns included the abolition of child labour in 1908.

4   Article 12 is no longer active in England but its work continues through the Children's Rights Alliance for England (CRAE). There is an Article 12 group in Scotland.

5   Concluding observations of the UN Committee on the Rights of the Child: 1995 in relation to the UK's 1st report, CRC/C/15Add.34; 2002, in relation to the UK's 2nd report, CRC/C/15/Add.188.

# 3 The practice of advocacy: Participation, voice and resistance

[The advocate explained to social services that] Sunna doesn't want to be split up from her baby and she doesn't want to go back to her family . . . And they said I can't care about him (the baby), but I can. My aunty (foster carer) helps me . . . they said I have to go to court to see what the judge says. And then we went to court and the judge said that the mother and baby should stay together. The judge said, take a residence order for the baby, and they can stay in foster care long-term.

(Sunna, 17-year-old young Asian woman with a learning disability,
in Knight and Oliver 2007: 420)

## Introduction

From the analysis so far, we can see that the landscape in which advocacy has evolved is complex. Contested concepts of childhood, children's rights and changing patterns of welfare, alongside increasing surveillance, closer regulation of young people's lives and bureaucratic delivery of services has impacted on debates about advocacy practice. Advocacy is also developing within a policy agenda promoting the participation of children and young people in health, welfare and education. It has become established as a way of promoting children's participation, voice and resistance. However, the participation agenda and issues around voice also feed into advocacy and how it is understood. It has been argued that bearing in mind the powerful adult agendas that inevitably impact on how far children and young people are able to participate, 'having a say is insufficient' (Clark and Percy-Smith 2006: 2). The expansion of advocacy provision within this context makes it timely to consider the complexities of participation, voice and advocacy. This is necessary both to open up critical dialogue about advocacy policy and practice, and to ensure that developing knowledge about advocacy is interrogated. Understanding of advocacy therefore needs to be informed by how the concepts of participation and voice impact on advocacy if advocates are to engage with and inform the constantly changing situations within which they operate. We therefore begin this chapter by examining developing understandings about participation before going on to consider the concept of voice in order to explore how advocacy is constructed within these contested areas.

## Participation

> Most professionals are intimidating – they have so much more power than you. When you are a 14 year old girl at school and you are trying to put your point across you are right down there and they are all the way up there.
>
> (Jasmine, age 14, in Maze Evaluation 2008)

In earlier chapters, we have contextualized how children's and young people's participation has become increasingly prominent in policy and practice initiatives within the UK. While many of these primarily relate to consultation with children and young people or their involvement as service users in decision-making processes (Kirby 1999; Kirby and Bryson 2002), discourses of participation are central to the development of advocacy and, in relation to children and young people, are influenced by the discourses of childhood and rights. Participation has been described as 'the keystone of the arch that is the United Nations Convention on the Rights of the Child' (Badham 2002: 6). The term 'participation' is problematic however, as it means different things to different people, and although participation has been considered a desirable goal for some time, the term has not been clearly defined (Murray and Hallett 2000). Nevertheless, participatory practice is often associated with key values such as user control and leadership, trust and respect, equality between professionals and service users and mutuality (Healy 1998). Murray and Hallett (2000) remind us, though, that participation rights usually exist because the right to self-determination is absent – that is, if children and young people had the right to self-determination, the right to participate would not be necessary, as is the case for many adults.

The exercise in Box 3.1 is designed to enable us to think about barriers and bridges to participation and to begin the process of thinking about what participation means from the perspectives of children, young people and adults. In essence, participation means 'taking part in' and has been defined by Hart in his essay on participation as 'The process of sharing decisions which affect one's life and the life of the community in which one lives' (Hart 1992: 5). This means that both children/young people and adults have the opportunity to work together to make decisions and essentially advocacy involves advocates working with children and young people to facilitate this process. Practices

---

**Box 3.1**   Exercise: Participation

---

Think of a time when you have successfully promoted the participation of a child or young person in a decision-making process (this may be in a personal or professional capacity).

- What enabled the involvement of the young person?
- What barriers did you have to overcome?
- What would you say was the young person's view of this process?
- What would you say were the adults' views of this process?

---

based on this ideal have been described as 'maintaining a balance between the powers of statutory agencies to determine the social conditions in which people live, and the empowerment of citizens to avoid encroachment on the living conditions they establish for themselves' (Sainsbury 1989: 106). If applied to children and young people, this assumes that they have the status of citizens – participation referring to the autonomy of children and young people to take actions and make choices as active citizens. Participation can then be described as a process that provides a structure for children's and young people's decision making but goes beyond the formal decision-making processes. However, other structures are also in place to enable adult professionals to make decisions – often deemed to be in the best interests of children and young people – which arguably fail to provide an adequate space to facilitate their participation in that process. In formal decision-making processes, the imperative to involve children and young people in the processes of making decisions about their lives can be difficult without advocacy support (Boylan 2008; Dalrymple and Horan 2008b). The level and nature of participation for children and young people in such decision-making processes can vary from 'taking part in' or 'being present at', to knowing that children's and young people's actions and views are taken into account and acted on (Department of Health 2001b).

## Ideological approaches to participation

In response to debates about participation, two broad ideological approaches have emerged with different underpinning philosophies: the consumerist/managerial approach to participation and the democratic approach (Braye 2000; Beresford 2005). The consumerist/managerial approach to participation developed in the latter part of the twentieth century with the increasing use of market approaches within health and social care services. In the late 1970s, emphasis on purchasing services meant that people using health and social care services became reframed as active consumers. Their 'needs' were recognized and the responsiveness, accessibility and quality of services were emphasized. Participation or service user involvement therefore meant 'improving the product' by obtaining feedback from customers in various ways to improve economy, efficiency and effectiveness. The view here is that consumers can and should exercise what could be described as a 'buying power' over services. If they are not actually paying directly for the service, they should at least be able to choose service providers and challenge standards. The core principles of consumerism, embedded in policy and practice relating to health and social care, are accessibility, information, choice and redress. This means for children and young people that:

- the focus is on the individual child or young person and their use of a particular service;
- services may become more responsive and relevant but effectively are still owned and controlled by the service provider; and
- children and young people can address concerns of access, information, choice and complaint about a service.

Clearly, the consumerist perspective underpins the introduction of complaints procedures under the Children Act 1989. The subsequent legal mandate for children and young people to be provided with access to advocacy support when making a complaint is therefore influenced by consumerist approaches to participation.

Hirschman (1970) provides a framework of 'exit', 'voice' and 'loyalty' to explain the options available to consumers if they are to influence the market system (Box 3.2). This model distinguishes the one-way relationship of exit and loyalty from the more interactive process of voice – but they are also related. A consumer who is dependent on limited access to an essential service may be unwilling to use voice to express dissatisfaction if opportunities to go elsewhere are not easily available. For example, children and young people living away from home in residential settings, foster care, boarding schools or as long-stay hospital patients are less likely to complain about their care when they have nowhere else to go. It is recognition of this imperative that has led to the legal mandate for children and young people to have access to an advocate when making a complaint under the Children Act 1989. Equally, a service may be more likely to listen to the voice of its 'customers' when there is a realistic possibility of losing them to competitors. For example, a local authority may be more likely to listen to foster carers who they do not want to lose to a private fostering service. The expression of voice, however, may also be limited by feelings of loyalty to the service/product. For example, a young person may not want to appear disloyal to a key worker, foster carer or teacher with whom they have a good relationship. Or voice may effectively be silenced by organizations preferring to encourage exit rather than deal with troublesome 'customers', as has happened when young people have been moved from one residential setting to another. In such circumstances, advocacy is needed to enable the consumer voice to be heard.

The consumerist approach has been described as 'an uneasy foundation for public welfare' (Braye 2000: 18), with factors such as eligibility criteria, agency defensiveness, resource constraints, commissioning advocacy services through service level agreements, and professional control of complaints and representation procedures constraining and limiting its impact (Braye and Preston-Shoot 1995). The consumerist perspective has also been criticized for supporting the 'managerialist' element of participation and service user involvement (Beresford 2005; Boylan and Braye 2006). Beresford points out that since 1997 when the New Labour government came into power, there has been increasing emphasis on the managerialist role of user involvement in activities such as audit and inspection alongside other provision for participation in planning, individual assessment, complaints procedures and, through consultation, the management of services.

Applying this model to children and young people, we see children viewed as consumers and stakeholders, with inherent claims of choice and redress. However, as Boylan and Braye (2006) have noted, there is an assumption that mechanisms for redress such as representation and complaints procedures are

---

**Box 3.2**  Hirschman's model

Exit:      Consumers can stop using a service and go elsewhere, as long as there are accessible alternatives. This is not an option easily available to children and young people, even with the support of an advocate.

Voice:    Consumers can try to influence the service by expressing an opinion using a complaints system, opportunities for consultation, etc. The Children Act 1989 gives children and young people looked after in local authority care the right to complain. Recognizing that this is not an easy process the Children Act 2004 provides children and young people with the legislative mandate for access to independent advocacy support if they are making a complaint under the Children Act 1989.

Loyalty:  Even though they may not be completely satisfied with the service consumers may continue to use it without complaint because of considerations such as convenience, vulnerability or commitment to the product. For children and young people living away from home their vulnerability, or commitment to a particular foster carer or key worker for example, may mean that this is their option of choice.

adequate. The complaints process was intended to be accessible, easily understood and to operate within a spirit of cooperation between the child and the local authority (Department of Health 1991). While not denying the importance of representation and complaints procedures as mechanisms for redress, in practice research indicates that they fail to provide an appropriate mechanism for children and young people to express concerns or to make a complaint (Ward 1995; Utting 1997; Aiers and Kettle 1998; Boylan and Boylan 1998; Wallis and Frost 1998; Bridge 1999; Children's Commissioner for Wales 2005; Pithouse and Crowley 2006). As we discussed in Chapter 1, such concerns echo earlier successful calls (Lindsay 1991) for independent advocacy and complaints procedures. Current representation and complaints mechanisms effectively leave institutional power and organizational structures challenged but unchanged. This is reflected in young people's views about complaints procedures, which indicate that they continue to experience difficulties when trying to make a complaint:

- Complaints procedures should be '*quick and easy*',
- Anyone hearing a complaint should '*listen and take action*', and
- Social service should always '*sort it out*'.

(Morgan 2008: 23)

The democratic approach to participation, however, has its roots in service user movements, particularly movements of disabled people. Croft and Beresford (1995) suggest that the power of the citizen is greater if it evolves through self-advocacy and experience. There are clear links here with debates about children's and young people's self-determination and autonomous decision making (Franklin 2002). The democratic approach focuses on ensuring that people have an influence in relation to the services that they are using and the organizations that impact on them (including policy making, resource allocation and management) so that they have more control over their lives (Beresford 2005). This approach concentrates on:

- provision of services for all;
- fairness and justice;
- citizen rights and responsibilities;
- collective action; and
- agenda setting as well as responding.

The democratic approach to participation therefore enables young people to influence the decisions that affect their lives. The focus is on participatory rights to be heard, participate, exercise choice and define problems and action. Many forms of advocacy have their roots in this approach to participation, as we shall see in the following chapter.

However, participation is dependent on the operation of wider power relations that may frustrate or distort the desired outcomes. Since the democratic approach aims to change service users' experience of service delivery collectively, rather than individually, it has been described as a political approach to involvement (Beresford 2005) because its main concern is to ensure that service users are able to promote change directly. This is particularly relevant to thinking about systemic advocacy.

## Models of participation

Theoretical debates about participation have generally been in terms of models that focus on the mechanisms and systems that have been devised to promote the inclusion of children and young people in various decision-making processes. These are designed to enable conceptual analysis of what have been seen as different levels or degrees of participation. For advocates working to involve children and young people in decision-making processes, the level of participation may vary from full participation in the process, based on an understanding that they have an equal and valid contribution to make, to what may be seen as a more 'tickbox' approach based on a young person's response on a form asking if their wishes and views have been sought.

Hart's (1992) metaphorical ladder of participation (Box 3.3) is a reconfiguration of Arnstein's (1969) model, based on the premise that power and participation are inextricably linked. It has been suggested that for its time Arnstein's ladder was ground-breaking, presenting practitioners with a model to reflect on their practice and develop more radical ways of working – to consider whether they were working in an effective participatory way or whether in fact they were agents of social control (Barber and Naulty 2005). Furthermore, Barber and Naulty point out that the model has played an important role in facilitating debate about participation.

Hart's adaptation of the ladder also provides a framework for advocates and professionals working in health, education and social welfare to reflect critically on the extent to which policy and practice are participatory. It can be used to open up a dialogue with young people about their experiences of participation and barriers. Hart's model was intended as a tool for community-based participation, and the various rungs of the ladder reflect a range of participatory options depending on the circumstances. He uses eight levels of participation, comprising in ascending order: manipulation, decoration, tokenism, assigned but not uninformed, consulted and informed, adult initiated, shared decisions with children and young people, child initiated and directed, child initiated, and shared decisions with adults.

Shier (2001) has developed a model that moves the emphasis from the young person to the organization. Shier's model has been embraced as a key

**Box 3.3** Hart's ladder of participation

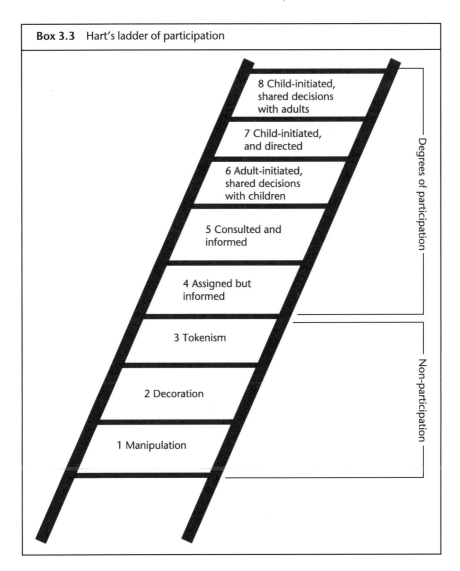

theoretical model that aims to enable adults working with children and young people to enhance their participation across five levels: children are listened to, children are supported in expressing their views, children's views are taken into account, children are involved in decision making and children share power and responsibility for decision making. His model, *pathways to participation*, begins with listening to children and young people and moves to developing policy and practice that facilitates this. It focuses on the willingness of organizations to involve children and young people, with three stages of commitment at each level: openings, opportunities and obligations. Fifteen questions can be used by workers and organizations to assess the current position, the goal and what needs to be done to achieve the goal.

The first stage is when an opening occurs and a worker or organization identifies an interest and a readiness to operate at that level, for example making a commitment to ensure that children and young people have access to advocacy. It is simply an *opening* because there may not be an opportunity to make it happen. The second stage occurs when there is an opportunity to work at this level in practice, for example funding is obtained to set up an advocacy service or specialist skills are acquired to work with young people with particular communication needs. The third stage is when an obligation is established and this becomes agreed policy within an organization, for example a local authority commits to the provision of advocacy which then becomes part of the culture of the provision of children's services. Revisting the model Shier (2007) notes that the arrows on his original diagram suggest a *single pathway*, which contradicts the title of the model. Box 3.4 therefore indicates how this model has been amended to reflect the reality of how organizations work, and the many pathways to participation.

Both Hart's ladder and Shier's pathways to participation have been criticized for the implication that the lower levels should be avoided and that progression to the higher levels is the desired outcome. Various attempts have been made to adapt Hart's ladder. For example, Treseder and Crowley (2001) used the concept of a wheel with varying degrees of power depicted as spokes that may be applicable to a particular young person on a certain issue at an instant in time. The child or young person will move around the wheel as necessary. However, Shier (2006) notes that while we do use a ladder to get to the top in order to move on, we also often want to stop on a rung half way up the ladder to be at the right height for the job being undertaken, such as painting a window frame. He points out that while only half way up the ladder, it would not be helpful in such circumstances to climb higher, while without the ladder it would not be possible to complete the job: 'A set of rungs, however well-crafted, is of little use without the frame that connects them together' (Shier 2006: 18). Children or young people who are participating fully in decision-making processes where they are advocating for themselves may well be sharing power and responsibility with adults. But equally, children and young people may not always want to or feel able to participate at that level – therefore they may choose to be at a different level on the ladder, having worked with an advocate who will present their point of view, for example, while they take a less active part in the process. For an advocate, understanding the theory of participation means that they are less likely to move into non-participatory ways of working – for example, talking to other professionals without informing the young person concerned. This is an important element of good advocacy practice for young people: [The advocate] always checks if

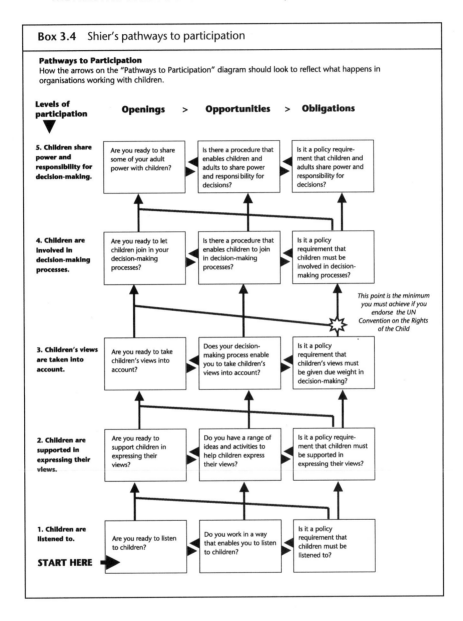

**Box 3.4** Shier's pathways to participation

it is OK with me if she is going to talk to someone which is nice' (Poppy, in Evaluation of Maze Advocacy Project 2008: 17).

A third model of participation is that of a bridge. This has been used by Taylor and Upward (1995) to demonstrate effective user involvement in community care and by John (1996) to demonstrate the politics of participation for young people. John argues for this more dynamic model because it encompasses 'the construction of creative alliances with adults which forms the true basis of an emotional democracy on which, it could be argued, children's participation must be based' (John 1996: 16). In her critique of Hart's ladder, she points out that his model is one in which rights are 'bestowed' on less powerful members of a community by the powerful. Arguing that the rights discourse is more about transforming power rather than helping less powerful people into the world of 'the dominant majority' (John 1996: 15), she suggests the need to go beyond models that originate from the ideologies of consumer involvement and draws on models emerging from the struggles of minority rights groups.

If children and young people are considered to be a minority rights group, John suggests bridge building is needed to bring together the world of children and young people and the adult world. The starting point for children and young people is to build a strong political movement for themselves. Having done this they are then in a position to build the bridge to cross the chasm between the two worlds and act together with adults in various ways, taking part in negotiation and collaborative activities. The flow across the bridge needs to be developed in both directions through events, projects or new groupings. The strength of the bridge depends on the time, resources and personnel allowed to develop it, how far the agendas of both sides allow flexibility, and how far it reaches out to the community of young people on one side and decision-making processes on the other. The bridge therefore needs firm foundations and ongoing maintenance. The maintenance can be undertaken by individuals or collaboratively, with all parties negotiating together in a process where the young people are not passive but active constructors and maintainers. This model is significant because it considers the role of adults and how power is negotiated and shared.

A more recent model of participation, which can usefully be adapted to working with children and young people in relation to advocacy, is the dialogical 'social learning' model of participation developed by Barry Percy-Smith (2006). His model also emanates from critiques of the first two approaches. Through his work with young people in community development, Percy-Smith uses principles of action research and participatory inquiry to develop an approach through dialogue based on lived experience. Rather than a process prescribed by adult professionals, this democratic model is based on communication between all participants. Percy-Smith draws on the work of Kemmis (2001) and Wildemeersch et al. (1988), identifying a key element of the process as a *communicative action space* in which adults are co-enquirers or interpretive learners with the young person rather than acting in their 'best interests'. Fundamental to the model is recognition that the differential power relations that exist between the various actors involved as a result of social and organizational relationships – children and young people, advocates, key adults in the lives of the children and young people and professionals – are central to enabling learning. Power, he notes, is negotiated rather than being given or taken away. Flexibility, mutual respect and reciprocity are therefore essential aspects of the process of participation:

> The assumption underlying reciprocity in communicative action spaces is that through dialogue and exchange, those involved are able to develop creative answers to the challenges at hand that are meaningful to the different parties involved.
>
> (Percy-Smith 2006: 169)

This model identifies the need for advocates to consider the type of spaces in which children and young people can participate and to be prepared to allow for learning between all those involved in the decision-making processes concerning children and young people.

Percy-Smith's (2006) model alerts us to the importance of taking account of the social, organizational and systemic contexts that children and young people are participating within. He also notes that young people's views are presented within a plurality of voices and value systems. Within these systems, the effects of dominant discourses of participation may hinder participatory processes in particular areas of practice. Examining the effects of discourse about participation on child protection practice, Healy (1998) suggests that

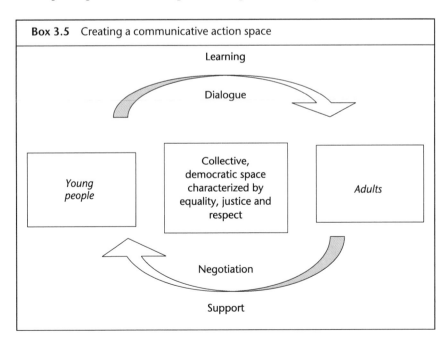

**Box 3.5**    Creating a communicative action space

Learning

Dialogue

Young people

Collective, democratic space characterized by equality, justice and respect

Adults

Negotiation

Support

the notion of participation in health and social work practice has been imported from various other disciplines (such as community development, social planning) and from social movements (such as feminism). This limits the development of participatory practice in areas of work such as child protection because it is based on an understanding that there is a set of universal practice implications accompanying participation that takes no account of context. Furthermore, she argues that the oppositional pairing of participation and paternalism denies the complex power relations that are inherent in child protection work. Her consideration of participatory practice that is responsive to the power relations that exist in the context of child protection can be applied to any discussion that addresses the participation of children and young people in an adult world and is reflected in the model proposed by Percy-Smith.

## Voice and resistance

> As soon as there is a power relation, there is a possibility of resistance. We can never be ensnared by power: We can always modify its grip in determinant conditions and according to a precise strategy.
>
> (Foucault 1988: 38)

The relevance of Foucault's work to advocacy is in his exploration of the way individuals are constructed as subjects, rather than power itself. Children and young people are not given power but it is constituted through discourse and practice. Our earlier discussions examining the social construction of childhood and debates around child care policy echo this point. Foucault argues that institutions, such as social services, health and education, have a physical presence, for example the classroom or a residential children's home. Institutions must also be understood as a set of constituted relationships between the various individuals, such as parents, teachers, social workers and those working in health. Their authority is gained from their status as 'guardians of truth', reinforced and legitimized by professional expertise and knowledge and legal determinations such as the 'best interests' paradigm discussed in Chapter 1. Significantly, dominant 'truths' inform the way that professionals understand and respond to children and young people as well as influencing the way children and young people see themselves.

As advocacy has developed and understandings of concepts of power have influenced practice, we can see that Foucault's analyses of power offers an alternative to thinking about how power is experienced and exercised (Chambon 1999) and therefore how children and young people can come to voice. The discourses of voice emanate from concerns that those who have been absent, unheard or silenced need space to be heard. In her examination of dilemmas in representing the voices of children in research, Alldred (1998) explores the political discourse of voice. She follows Spivak's (1988) distinction between representation meaning proxy and representation meaning advocacy, suggesting that for researchers the two may not be clearly distinguished. Alldred suggests that discourses of 'giving voice' enable children to be active subjects rather than objects and that research is one way of providing a space for those whose opinions are rarely heard. She goes on to identify the tensions that can arise in the ethnographic study of children, which challenge 'the general assumption that adults' benevolent attempts to represent children (as proxy or advocate) are necessarily always in their interests, and the simplicity with which it is assumed that what children say can be represented (portrayed) through research' (Alldred 1998: 151).

This raises two key issues for advocacy. The first is the notion of 'giving voice'; the second is that of representation. The assumption that adults might be able to 'give' children and young people a voice is problematic. Maguire (2001) notes a caution by Noffke (1998) against the notion of 'giving' voice, suggesting that 'we must see ourselves as part of the process of breaking apart the barriers for speakers and listeners, writers and readers' (Maguire 2001: 10). Enabling children and young people to 'come to voice' (hooks 1989) is therefore a more helpful way of understanding advocacy practice. Code (2000: 192) suggests that *'practices of advocacy often make knowledge possible* within the hierarchical distributions of autonomy and authority within western societies' (original emphasis). Such an understanding of advocacy means that children and young people using services may often require the guidance of adults to know what their experiences are. Advocacy makes 'truths available for negotiation' (Code 2000: 18) with, by and for children, young people, their advocates and adults involved in their lives and so, Code states, 'advocacy can counter-balance the patterns of incredulity into which the testimony of marginalised knowers tends to fall' (p. 18). For her, advocacy is well placed to put 'knowledge into circulation where it can claim acknowledgement and working to ensure informed, emancipatory moral-political effects' (p. 19).

Understanding advocacy as making knowledge possible enables a response to ethical concerns against adults speaking for children and young people. Arguments by writers such as bell hooks (1994), that the representation of oppressed groups by dominant groups can erase their 'voice', are powerful. Equally powerful is the recognition that 'not to speak about or for "others" encourages silences and gaps, which marginalise and exclude, while cementing the privilege of those with the more powerful voices' (Gillies 2005: 54). Consideration also needs to be given to the relationship between voice and audience, particularly as the voices of children and young people may often not be listened to or the 'significance of their words is denied' (Hoggett 2000: 41). Therefore, alongside the development of advocacy, which is enabling children and young people to 'speak' in their own voice, the adult audience 'needs to learn to hear in new ways' (Hoggett 2000: 115). Failing to hear children's voices is an act of adult resistance. Coming to voice represents the opportunity for counter-resistance by children and young people. Therefore, resistance can be perceived as a way of exercising power to resist those in dominant positions.

Acts of resistance by children and young people may include:

- contacting an advocate for support;
- refusing to attend or participate in a meeting (for example, a statutory review meeting, child protection conference);
- campaigning against a particular policy/practice;
- refusing to sign daily record sheets or complete review consultation booklets;
- challenging decisions they have not been involved in reaching;
- making a complaint;
- refusing medication;
- questioning the purpose of assessment; and
- running away.

The situation of Tim (Box 3.6) is an example of the relational nature of power and the possibility of resistance. The first act of resistance, Hoggett suggests, is for children and young people to 'find, develop or recover their voice' (Hoggett 2000: 114). Tim first tried to 'find' his voice through the mechanism of the representations and complaints procedure. He met with counter-resistance and attempts to suppress his voice. The role of advocacy within that process was to facilitate the 'recovery' of voice. It could also be regarded as an example of the officer in charge attempting to exercise absolute power.

## Summary

An awareness of the concepts of participation, voice and resistance can help advocates understand the complex situations they are likely to encounter in their daily practice. Understanding the power relations that exist between children and young people and the range of professionals they come in to contact with as part of their daily lives is the starting point for developing a 'communicative action space' within which to enable children and young people's participation. Despite critiques about some participatory methods of working (Cooke and Kothari 2001; Percy-Smith and Malone 2001; Kirby et al. 2003; Hickey and Mohan 2004; Tisdall and Davies 2004), the case for promoting the participation rights of children and young people is clear:

> Promoting children and young people's participation helps to counter their invisibility as people. It brings their needs and views to the

---

**Box 3.6**   Case study: Tim

---

Tim, aged 16, is looked after by Crosscountry local authority. For the past six months he has lived in a small local authority residential children's home. Tim had seen posters encouraging looked after children and young people to express their views and opinions – the posters assured young people their views were import-ant and they would be listened to. Information was also provided about the representations and complaints procedure, which emphasized that any com-plaint made would be treated with respect. Tim did have a complaint and so he confidently wrote this down and took it to the officer in charge. Having given the complaint to the officer in charge, Tim was invited in to 'the office' where his complaint was shredded in front of him. Nothing was said to Tim as he was escorted from the office. Tim talked to another young person about what had happened who suggested that he could talk to the independent advocate who regularly visited the residential unit. The advocate met with Tim and supported him to make another complaint, which was taken seriously.

---

regular attention of adults and helps transform negative attitudes and behaviour. Increased visibility should lead us away from seeing chil-dren as people-in-the-making, simply passing time until they enter adulthood, towards respecting them as complete human beings with needs, feelings and evolving capacities from the moment they are born.

(Willow 2002: 37)

The concept of voice is central to promoting children's participation and their democratic rights. It is a political action. Key to the process of participa-tion is the ability to develop and articulate one's voice. Hence the impor-tance of moving from thinking about enabling children and young people to develop and articulate voice, to thinking about enabling their 'coming' to voice. It is only then, when children and young people can use the communi-cation space created through working with an advocate that the opportunities for participation and resistance become possible. The metaphor of voice is common to feminist and action research. Participatory research, for example, is about the right to speak and argues for the articulation of views by the dominated. By listening to children and young people, we can gain the infor-mation we need for a fuller understanding of the issues that affect their lives. By dealing with voices we are affecting power relations. To listen to people is to empower them. Butler and Rumsey suggest that this:

Probably provides the single most important clue as to why there is such resistance to meaningful dialogue with children. If we were to really listen to children and hear what they have to say, it would result in the need to radically change many of the services that are currently provided. While they are ostensibly designed to enhance the well being of children, in practice it could be argued that they are organised around the desire to maintain the current position of children in society and existing power relationships.

(Butler and Rumsey 2000: 15)

If children and young people are to come to voice, the starting point for advocates is to continue to make visible the paradoxical discourses, which come from the exercise of adult power. Hoggett (2000) explores the link between the process of empowerment and the process of 'becoming conscious of', or 'conscientization'. Examining how workers in the welfare state deprive people of their voice through forms of institutional disempowerment, he argues that central to this process is the ability to develop and articulate one's voice. Advocacy has shown that breaking down barriers for speakers and listeners, perpetuated through adult-designed and adult-led service for children and young people which act to support the position of adults, has the potential to enable children and young people to participate and have a voice in decision making.

# 4 What is advocacy and who defines it?

Child advocacy actually has to do with a state of mind or an attitude character-
ised by a faith in the competence of children. Accordingly, as an academic or
as a practitioner, on whatever level, the point of departure for an advocate for
children is the viewpoint of the child, for example, what are the child's experiences, feelings and opinions. We must have confidence in the ability of children to express their views and allow them to have an impact on the situation
wherever possible. This attitude also bridges the gap between theory and
practice.

(Flekkoy 1993, in Harvey 1993: 30)

## Introduction

An answer to the question 'what is advocacy' will bring diverse answers
depending on, for example, personal and professional experience, knowledge,
values and policy agendas. Fixed definitions can be limiting and must be
understood in the context of the definer and the purpose for which they are
written. For example, a definition of advocacy from a young person is likely to
be different from that of a doctor, teacher or social worker. However, it is also
important to critically examine how advocacy is defined because 'constituen-
cies or differences in understanding are likely to influence advocacy practice as
well as stakeholder responses to it' (Oliver et al. 2006). Definitions inevitably
come from a range of sources – some from children and young people, others
from (adult) service user groups and various professional bodies and central
and local government organizations. In this chapter, we therefore try to cap-
ture the essence of the concept of advocacy through discussion of various
definitions. Before considering these, however, the exercise in Box 4.1 is a
useful starting point to examine understandings of advocacy.

Having completed this activity, you will see that definitions of advocacy
range from declarations about the practice of advocacy (in the first statement)

---

**Box 4.1** Exercise: Advocacy definitions

---

Consider what you like and dislike about the following definitions. Decide which one you like best and think about why.

1 'Giving voice to the voiceless.'
2 'Using one or several of many ways to represent the person's views, interests and wishes as if they were the advocate's own.'
3 'Those elements of activities, services and processes which provide supportive representation and weighting for the wishes, needs, values and perspectives of a person or group.'
4 'Supporting users to speak, and persuading services to shut up and listen.'
5 'Advocacy is taking action to help people say what they want, secure their rights, represent their interests and obtain services they need. Advocates and advocacy schemes work in partnership with the people they support and take their side. Advocacy promotes social inclusion, equality and social justice.'
6 'Advocacy is concerned with getting one's needs, wants, opinions and hopes taken seriously and acted upon. It can take a number of different forms including self-advocacy, citizen advocacy, and patient advocacy . . . advocacy is essential because it allows people to participate more fully in society by expressing their own viewpoints, by participating in management and decision making and by availing of rights to which they are entitled.'

(Exercise reprinted by kind permission from Michele Winter,
Bristol City Social Services Training Dept.)

---

to understandings that reflect the principles and values of advocacy (in the last two). The focus on the definition may depend on whether the definer is a young person, an advocate or a commissioner of advocacy services. However, all the definitions have key components, which to varying degrees include elements of voice, representation and rights. When children and young people are denied the ability to speak up freely for their interests, there is a need for them to have access to advocacy support. However, there are different understandings about advocacy, which are reflected in contemporary debates about what constitutes advocacy. Through an examination of various definitions we intend to explore different views about the nature of advocacy rather than seeking any fixed definition. We will begin to examine its contested nature by relating to theoretical perspectives, service user mandates and legislative imperatives.

## Exploring definitions

> Advocacy is the act of speaking in support of human concerns or needs. Where people have their own voice advocacy means making sure they are heard; where they have difficulty speaking up it means providing help; where they have no voice it means speaking for them.
>
> (Herbert 1989: 49)

Before examining the term advocacy in depth, we need to locate the discussion within a framework of advocacy practice. The term advocacy has been used to refer to work with individual children and young people that may involve working on particular issues but may also have a wider remit aimed at broader structural changes relating to legislation, policy or practice. Clarke (2003) describes three generic practices that usefully summarize these divisions:

- Issue-based advocacy (also referred to as case advocacy by some writers) is a task-centred way of working where an advocate works with a child or young person on a particular issue.
- Relationship-based advocacy is where an advocate works with a child or young person on a long-term basis (such as citizen advocacy – see Chapter 5; but could also fall into the issue-based category here).
- General-issue advocacy where an advocate may campaign on wider structural issues or support groups to do so (this form of advocacy is also known as cause, systemic or public policy advocacy).

We have chosen to use the term *issue-based advocacy* throughout the book to refer to advocacy with individual children and young people and *systemic advocacy* to refer to advocacy in relation to macro issues. In exploring definitions, we will begin by focusing on individual issue-based advocacy from children's and young people's perspectives.

## Speaking up – advocacy and individuals

> Advocates should always listen to you and your opinions, and put your point of view across . . . whether he thinks you are right or not.
>
> (Young person, in Morgan 2008: 22)

Research indicates that children and young people have a clear view about what constitutes advocacy (Oliver and Dalrymple 2008). Recurring themes in the literature point to the importance of advocates being able to listen to and speak up for young people as identified in the quotation from the young person above. Advocacy in this respect can be undertaken by any professional working with children and young people. The case example taken from *Getting it Right for Every Child* (Creegan et al. 2006) is a useful example of the nature of the advocacy role within social work (see Box 4.2).

The quotations from young people in Box 4.3 also suggest that there is something about the advocacy relationship that is unique and distinctive. While this is possible within a range of relationships that children and young people might have with a trusted adult, for those young people who seek advocacy support it is arguably more likely that the young person who felt 'free' had felt inhibited in other relationships with adults. Furthermore, we can see that there is a tension between the professional obligation to work within a best interests framework and some aspects of the advocacy role. It is apparent in the definition above, for example, that a feature of the advocate's role that is important to young people is that the advocate also steps back from the 'best

---

**Box 4.2**   Case study: Jade

The case of Jade, aged 14, provides an example of a supportive type of relationship with a social worker, who as a result was able to play a central role in providing advocacy support in the Hearings[1] system. Jade likened her relationship with her social worker to that of a friend, who listened to her:

> 'It's just I don't see [her] as a social worker. I see [her] as a friend because of the way she listens and that . . . I can talk to [her] and feel that she listens, but when it was the other ones, I didn't feel as though they listened to me'.

Both Jade and her social worker, who saw herself as an advocate for Jade, explained that their relationship had been built up over time. The fact that she had previously been involved with Jade's family meant that she was known and trusted by both Jade and her mother. The relationship that Jade had developed with her was contrasted positively to that with previous social workers. Her social worker's approach was to work with her closely in the run up to a Hearing, enabling Jade to comment on a draft of the report that was to be presented to the Hearing. Jade was able to talk to her if she felt nervous about the Hearing. The extent of Jade's confidence in her social worker and the importance attached to her role can be judged by the fact that on one occasion she said that she did not want a Hearing to go ahead because the social worker was not able to be present.

(Adapted from Creegan et al. 2006)

---

**Box 4.3**  Young people's understanding of advocacy

---

I don't know, she's just always there and she knows, she knows most about me than anybody else. (James, aged 14; Creegan et al. 2006: 22)

Advocacy is the act of arguing on behalf of a particular issue, idea or person. (Morgan 2008: 9)

An advocate is a person who listens to what you say and then speaks for you somewhere you are not comfortable or cannot otherwise be represented. (Morgan 2008: 9)

Advocacy is a person who helps children who are in care. They make sure the social worker is listening to them, that they're getting what they are entitled to, making sure they are not being abused in care, and helping if they have any complaints. (Ismail, aged 19)

They are there to help and their wishes and feelings don't come in to it . . . they may not agree with what the young person wants, but they still have to go along with that because that is what the young person's asking for. (Boylan 2005: 9)

Someone who will stick up for you, who turns up when they say they are going to and is your friend. (Boylan 2005: 9)

With her I felt free, not shy at all. Because we were only two so I was free to say out my views without any problem. (Dalyrimple 2005: 4)

---

interests' perspective – it is not whether the advocate agrees or disagrees, it is about creating the space to listen and put forward the views of the young person. In addition, young people's definitions of advocacy include an understanding that the advocacy role extends to more actively fighting their corner (Morgan 2008). Both these elements of advocacy cannot easily be undertaken by professionals working with children and young people and therefore support the case for independent advocacy.

Independence from service providers has been a consistent feature in the development of advocacy services. Longstanding concerns about the independence of advocacy for children and young people are reflected in the literature (Timms 1995; Smith and Ing 1996; Dalrymple 2001). This is also apparent in the wording of the National Standards for the Provision of Children's Advocacy Services (Department of Health 2002; Welsh Assembly Government 2003). Standard 6, *Advocacy Works Exclusively for Children and*

*Young People*, sends an important message about independence. Paragraph 6.1 states that: 'The advocacy service is as far as possible, funded and managed in a way that ensures independence from the commissioning body, so that children and young people have confidence that their advocates will act for them and are free from any conflicts of interest'.

Research suggests that children and young people have strong views about independence (Oliver et al. 2005; Crowley and Pithouse 2008; Morgan 2008). Boylan and Ing (2005) found that most looked after children and young people wanted advocates to be independent of the organization looking after them. They were also acutely aware of a potential conflict of interest between commissioners and advocacy providers where the relationship 'became too cosy'. The research also found a link between the advocate's degree of independence and their relationship with the young person. In the context of looked after children and young people, the degree of professional distance between the advocate and other residential staff was especially significant. For example, good advocates 'did not go into the office' or 'talk about you with other staff'. Keeping the roles separate and distinct was reassuring and a real sign of the advocate's independence. It was also felt to be a measure of the extent to which they could trust the advocate, even when they were mistrustful of others. The importance of independence and distance from the local authority in relation to the representation and complaints procedures is another key research finding (Oliver et al. 2005; Crowley and Pithouse 2008; Morgan 2008).

Commissioning arrangements can potentially pose a real challenge to the independence of advocacy providers. Advocacy services may be delivered in a range of ways, including by national voluntary organizations, by the local authority and by a local voluntary organization. These arrangements are further complicated by funding streams, which may include total funding from host local authorities, or a combination of funding from the local authority, with a 20–30 percent contribution from a voluntary organization, or a mix of funding from local authorities, health trusts, connexions services and the Big Lottery or other charitable sources (Oliver 2008). Over half of the advocacy services in Oliver's study received all of their funding from the host local authority

Clearly, there is a potential for Service Level Agreements (SLAs) or contracts between commissioners and advocacy providers to constrain or compromise the independence of the advocacy organizations, and the practice and integrity of individual advocates. Commissioning arrangements also have an impact in determining confidentiality thresholds in relation to advocacy for children and young people. Young people's definitions of advocacy appear to assume that the advocacy relationship is totally confidential: 'I could tell her (the advocate) anything about my personal life and I know she wouldn't say anything' (Sarah, in Boylan 2005: 196). This is important from the perspectives of children and young people who have identified it as an important element in informing their decision making concerning who they might talk to. However, research indicates that the need for confidentiality is more likely to be contested when providing advocacy for disabled children and young people. Adults have questioned the relevance of confidentiality, particularly for children and young people with complex communication needs and severe disabilities. In contrast, from disabled children's and young people's perspectives, the confidentiality that advocates offered is highly valued (Knight and Oliver 2007).

Throughout the UK, confidentiality is treated procedurally (Wattam 1999; Dalrymple 2001) and this has led to the development of confidentiality thresholds and policies in practice in health, education, social work and advocacy. In the UK, confidentiality operates within a best interests framework, and consequently professionals may breach confidentiality if, in doing so, it is deemed to be in the best interests of the child. This approach is reflected in Standard 7 of the National Standards for the Provision of Children's Advocacy Services, which requires that an advocacy service 'operates to a high level of confidentiality and ensures that children, young people and other agencies are aware of its confidentiality policies' (Department of Health 2002; Welsh Assembly Government 2003). Furthermore, advocacy services must have 'a clear confidential policy grounded in the concept of significant harm' (Department of Health 2002: 11). Confidentiality is therefore limited rather than absolute. The problem with this approach is that it may inhibit children and young people who wish to use an advocacy service where confidentiality is limited (Wattam 1999; Dalrymple 2001). A different approach is taken, however, by some European countries. In Finland, advocacy legislation exists to allow children and young people to access confidential services that operate an absolute confidentiality threshold. For example, the Ombudsman in Finland is 'bound to professional secrecy by law' (Molander 1996: 577). With the exception of Voices from Care in Wales, one of the few services to offer absolute confidentiality, such an approach could inform advocacy services for children and young people in a UK context.

## Empowerment

> When people are denied or unable to gain access to a fair share of what's on offer in society – when they are denied information or opportunities to take part in decisions concerning their lives – when they are dispossessed of insight, dignity, self confidence – then it becomes necessary in a caring society for more powerful people to act with integrity on their behalf or wherever possible to enable them to move to a point where they can retrieve control for themselves.
>
> (Advocacy in Action 1990)

This definition of advocacy provided by disabled adult service users is derived from their experiences of feeling powerless in a range of situations and resonates with the experiences of young people. However, this definition goes beyond locating advocacy practice within individual decision making to recognizing the oppression of marginalized groups in society and the impact this has on their capacity to control their own lives. The notion of 'more powerful' people acting on behalf of people needing advocacy support is worth unpacking a little more. If we think about power in the context of advocacy for children and young people, it is helpful to think about relational power – that is, power that is exercised with or alongside others. Pierson (2008) explains that this is expressed as 'power to' rather than 'power over' when advocates and young people work together to share ideas and agree on a course of action. For Pierson this is a process that takes time and involves the need to build advocacy relationships which is reflected in the young people's views on advocacy in Box 4.3. Achieving relational power involves the advocate recognizing and nurturing the strengths and capacities of children and young people. This process then facilitates moving from feeling 'dispossessed of insight, dignity and self confidence' towards 'a point where they can retrieve control for themselves'.

Power can also be understood in terms of instrumental power, which involves the exercise of power over one group by another. This is encapsulated in the following definition, which identifies the need for advocacy to challenge influential service providers who have the power to make people's lives worse through, for example, the closure of a residential unit, being moved from an established foster home or exclusion from school: 'Advocacy involves a person(s), either an individual or a group with disabilities or their representative, pressing their case with influential others, about situations which affect them directly or, and more usually, trying to prevent proposed changes which will leave them worse off' (Brandon 1995: 1).

While the concept of empowerment is implicit in the definitions that we have looked at so far, it is explicit in the following definition from Comhairle[2]:

> Advocacy, which has always existed in human relationships is a process of empowerment and can take many forms. It is a way of enabling those who may have difficulty speaking up for themselves to do so and thus can be key to involvement in decision making. It generally means representing the view of a person or supporting them to exercise or secure their rights.
>
> (Nua Research Services Report, in Weafer 2003: 7)

This definition also recognizes that advocacy is an enduring feature of human interactions in which any one may need or act as an advocate. However, we have already discussed the need for advocates to be independent of systems that disempower children and young people, which is identified in the following definition of advocacy:

> Many people in society are disempowered by systems which have a significant effect on almost every aspect of their lives. These are people who are disempowered to such an extent that they are unlikely to be able to fulfil their basic human needs, or demand their basic human rights. A person's initial hopes and dreams can be severely limited by this. Independent advocacy can help to widen a person's horizons and enable them to become active members of society
> (Advocacy 2000, 2002: 49)

Here the impact of disempowerment means that advocacy goes beyond the practical task enabling voice and agency to promoting active citizenship. This needs to be understood alongside the discourses of childhood, children's rights, participation, voice and resistance discussed in earlier chapters. The notion of children having a voice challenges adult/child power relations and early commentators have described advocacy as a 'controversial and politically daring practice' (McCall 1978: 41). For Melton (1987), who comments specifically on advocacy for children and young people, this more radical aim is clearly evident:

> To empower children, enabling them to make use of societal resources. Child advocates endeavor to raise the status of children and increase the responsiveness and accountability of the institutions affecting them. Advocacy consists of social action on behalf of children whether to increase their self-determination or to enhance the social, educational and medical resources to which they are entitled. Because it involves attempts to redistribute power to reallocate resources, child advocacy is inherently political.
> (Melton 1987: 357)

Here we see the definition emphasizes the need to raise the status of children and young people across all the services that children and young people encounter. Moreover, Melton recognizes the responsibility of social institutions in providing services for children and young people. His definition goes beyond ensuring that they can access the services that are available to ensuring that those services are fit for purpose and that professional structures are accountable. Advocacy therefore becomes an important tool in adjusting the power relations between service users and service providers (Braye and Preston-Shoot 1995; Tunnard 1997).

Empowerment can only be a component of advocacy, however, as not everyone experiences advocacy as an empowering process (Mickelson 1995).

Essentially, 'advocacy may be one part of a jigsaw of empowerment' and thus all an advocate may be able to do is to be part of enabling someone to fulfil their aims and wishes (Wiltshire Advocacy Project 1996). This is reflected in another early definition from the world's first Ombudsman for Children, Malfrid Grude Flekkoy: 'Child advocacy can be defined as a strategy . . . aimed at changing social systems, institutions and structures in order to maximise children's possibilities of self-determination' (Flekkoy 1991: 10).

The relationship that is established between an advocate and the person they are working alongside is central, particularly in relation to empowerment practice. We have already seen in young people's definitions of advocacy that the nature of the relationship is an essential element. This is identified in research that indicates that the close relationship established by many children and young people with their advocate is significant (Dalrymple and Oliver 2008). Bell (2002) reinforces this point in relation to children's rights, emphasizing the importance of building relationships as the foundation for meaningful engagement. The aim is to build an enabling relationship in which children and young people are given clear and accurate information, feel supported and are given the opportunity to voice their views and opinions. This requires a commitment of time and an approach that recognizes the value of children's voice and agency, as well as the incremental nature of building meaningful relationships with children and young people. Henderson and Pochin's definition encapsulates this feature:

> Advocacy can be described as the process of identifying with and representing a person's views and concerns, in order to secure enhanced rights and entitlements, undertaken by someone who has little or no conflict of interest. Put more positively, advocacy is rooted in a special, and perhaps unique, relationship between the advocate and the person they support.
>
> (Henderson and Pochin 2001: vi)

In summary, these definitions indicate that children and young people requiring advocacy may feel disempowered by the systems and processes that impact on their lives. As a result, they either need someone to speak (act) on their behalf or support to move towards a position of being able to advocate for themselves. Advocacy is facilitated by a trusting relationship with the child or young person concerned and independence of service providers. This is especially important if children and young people are to gain access to the services they need, clearly a simple but key function of advocacy with individual children and young people.

## Promoting change – advocacy and systems

There is a wider dimension to advocacy, however, in which it is also seen as a tool for challenging social injustice and as a means of promoting voice and agency. We saw above that advocacy has been described as politically daring and more recent definitions identify this political dimension of advocacy, locating it systemically, with a role to promote social awareness and the achievement of a more just society:

> A political act with consequences for both individuals and the com-
> munity as a whole, challenging inequality, opposing racism, prevent-
> ing abuse, or even introducing someone to a new opportunity or social
> setting – all constituting steps towards a more civil and just society.
>
> (Henderson and Pochin 2001: 15)

However, care needs to be taken not to over-state the reach of advocacy. For example, while the concept of advocacy as a safeguard for looked after young people is not new – having emerged from a legacy of abuse and failing to listen to children (Levy and Kahan 1991; Utting 1997; Waterhouse et al. 2000) – whether it could claim to 'prevent' abuse is debatable. Nevertheless, the need for looked after children and young people to be able to access independent forms of advocacy has been acknowledged, and legislation provides for them to have access to advocacy when making a complaint. Importantly, guidance in Working Together to Safeguard Children states that:

> Children and families may be supported through their involvement
> in safeguarding processes by advice and advocacy services, and they
> should always be informed of services that exist locally and nation-
> ally. Independent advocates provide independent and confidential
> information, advice and support and can play a vital role in ensuring
> children have appropriate information and support to communicate
> their views in formal settings, such as a child protection and court
> proceedings.
>
> (Department of Health 2006b: 5)

Although, this recognizes advocacy as part of a wider safeguarding strat-
egy, it does not identify it as a means of preventing abuse. However, the role of advocacy in 'opposing racism' can be more clearly articulated. Statistics (DfES 2006) indicate that there is continuing over-representation of black chil-
dren and young people of African and African-Caribbean origin looked after in public care. The role for advocacy here is to promote the visibility of black children's and young people's care experiences and enable their voices to be heard concerning the services they receive, which Graham (2007b: 1309)

argues will lead to 'more equitable and positive' outcomes. Through enabling black children and young people to come to voice, there is also the potential for advocates to challenge dominant discourses about black children and young people.

Advocacy for children and young people has been described as 'a social movement directed to the rights of children' (Paul 1977: 8), a description that fits well with the above definitions. Richart and Bing (1989) also emphasize systemic advocacy as the primary goal of advocacy services for children and young people – to initiate change in the systems that impinge on their lives. As early as 1989 they identified the importance of advocacy services combining both issue-based and systemic advocacy. These understandings of advocacy, however, are derived from advocacy initiatives in the United States and Canada, which provide a range of advocacy services closely linked to government-funded child and family advocacy centres and legal processes.

Nevertheless, the need for systemic advocacy within the service system is arguably a key element of advocacy practice in the UK. Systemic advocacy requires advocacy services to collate information about the effectiveness of child welfare systems, which, Richart and Bing (1989) argue, potentially can make central and local government agencies accountable to the children and young people for whom they are providing services. Directives from UK governments legislating for advocacy in particular situations recognize the significance of advocacy in relation to social justice. We see this, for example, in a definition by the Scottish Executive, which describes advocacy as 'a crucial element in achieving social justice. It is a way to ensure that everyone matters and everyone is heard – including people who are at risk of exclusion and people who have particular difficulties in making their views known' (Scottish Executive 2001: 1). Similarly, guidance for Independent Mental Capacity Advocates[3] states that:

> Advocacy promotes equality, social justice and social inclusion. It can empower people to speak up for themselves.
> Advocacy can help people become more aware of their own rights, to exercise those rights and be involved in and influence decisions that are being made about their future.
>
> (Lee 2007: 7)

The development of electronic advocacy (also known as Net-activism or e-advocacy) is particularly pertinent to promoting systemic change. Electronic advocacy 'refers to the use of high technology to influence the decision making process or to use technology in an effort to support policy change efforts' (Hick and McNutt 2002: 8). Hick and McNutt suggest that electronic advocacy uses internet-based technologies, uses 'new media' and compliments more traditional approaches to advocacy.

This definition of advocacy is linked to activism and has a role in providing information to advocates and practitioners and also in building bridges, organizing and mobilizing people through, for example, collaborative work in the community of advocates and with professionals to exchange information, identify common issues and lobby for change. Virtual advocacy communities can enable individuals to come together to influence policy making. Given that a lot of advocacy services are small or single-worker projects, e-advocacy enables information from issue-based advocacy to feed more easily into systemic advocacy and enables young people's experiences and voices to influence policy and practice. The problem here, though, is that despite its empowering potential there are limitations. Not all organizations or individuals have the same access to resources. In relation to technology, a lot of small advocacy services are unlikely to have the time, money, personnel, skills or access to training to go beyond issue-based advocacy and influence systemic change.

Acknowledging the link between advocacy, rights and social justice is a relatively recent development in the UK, although campaigning organizations have consistently argued that advocacy and rights are inevitably linked. For example, an early advocacy service for children and young people described advocacy as 'the activity of achieving rights for children' (Dalrymple 1993: 12). Nearly a decade later, we see that the Scottish Executive takes a similar view in relation to advocacy within the context of health services:

> Advocacy is the process of acting on behalf of another person to secure services or rights which they require or are entitled to. In the NHS it is an important way of enabling people to make informed choices and remain in control of their healthcare requirements. It also helps the patient gain access to information that may be needed and allows them to make their views and wishes known.
>
> (Scottish Executive 2001: 1)

There is an important distinction to be made here between the definition of advocacy from the service user organization Advocacy in Action discussed earlier and the Scottish Executive's definition above. In the former definition, service users express the desire to 'retrieve control' for themselves, whereas there is an assumption in the latter definition that as people are assisted to *remain* in control, then, in fact, control has never been lost. Children and young people may clearly feel that they have lost control in particular situations but at other times may be seeking to either gain more control or remain in control. When looking at definitions, therefore, it is important to be aware of the perspective of the definer. The definition in the National Standards for the Provision of Advocacy Services in England and Wales published by the respective governments in 2002–2003 is a case in point. In this definition, advocacy is seen as:

speaking up for children and young people. Advocacy is about empowering children and young people to make sure that their rights are respected and their views and wishes heard at all times. Advocacy is about representing the views, wishes and needs of children and young people to decision makers and helping them navigate the system.

(Department of Health 2002: 1; Welsh Assembly<br>Government 2003: 1)

This rather neutral definition places an emphasis on issue-based advocacy and working within *existing* systems. This is a far cry from Richart and Bing's (1989) assertion that systemic advocacy should have a key role in influencing how services are delivered and initiating changes in the provision of services to improve the lives of children. Nor does it in any way equate with Melton's (1987) vision of advocacy, which emphasizes social action in relation to children and young people. Essentially, this definition of passive advocacy (Jenkins 1995) fails to go beyond the individual and is inherently apolitical.

From these definitions of systemic advocacy, we see that there is the potential to offer a challenge to the dominant and powerful position of service providers and policy makers where appropriate. Advocacy can be seen to have a role to play in addressing the power relations between children and young people and health, social welfare and education providers. Advocacy can enable young people's views to contribute to shaping and informing services as well as challenging when necessary the professional power of organizations and practices that disadvantage or marginalize children and young people.

## Summary

In this chapter, we have captured the essence of the concept of advocacy through examining evolving definitions of advocacy from a range of sources. The starting point for thinking about advocacy is, as the quotation at the start of this chapter clearly asserts, 'on whatever level, the point of departure of an advocate for children is the viewpoint of the child'. This is relevant to both independent advocates and health, welfare and education professionals who have a commitment to children's rights and 'have it in their power to assist children in having a voice' (Hart 1992: 36). The definitions that we have looked at illustrate various perspectives about the nature of advocacy. Many of the definitions we have discussed indicate that advocacy is synonymous with the concepts of social justice, empowerment and autonomy. The roots of advocacy arise from marginalized groups, who, in seeking to come to voice and secure their rights, define advocacy from a radical perspective – both in relation to issue-based and systemic advocacy. Advocacy is therefore broadly defined as a method for enabling those who have previously been ignored or silenced to come to voice and to ensure that adults take what children and young people have to say seriously. It provides a possible force for change and the promotion of social justice.

In many ways, advocacy has emerged from the failings of services that actually espouse the same principles of challenging injustice. For example, the aims of social work are to promote:

> social change, problem solving in human relationships and the empowerment and liberation of people to enhance well-being. Utilising theories of human behaviour and social systems, social work intervenes at the points where people interact with their environments. Principles of human rights and social justice are fundamental to social work.
>
> (International Association of Schools of Social Work and
> International Federation of Social Workers 2001)

Within the current context of social work practice, such aims are not easy to achieve. Equally, advocacy is also becoming constrained through service level agreements and the imposition of national standards, so that in future the way that advocacy provision is defined and delivered is more likely to be influenced by rationing, budget constraints and bureaucracy. Definitions of advocacy incorporate understandings of the various forms of advocacy both at an individual and structural level. In the following two chapters, we consider how various forms of advocacy have emerged and explore models of advocacy provision to gain further insights into the complexity of the role of independent advocates alongside the advocacy role of professionals.

## Notes

1   Scotland's Children's Hearings system was initiated by the Social Work (Scotland) Act 1968. In 1971 children's hearings took over from the courts most of the responsibility for dealing with children & young people under 16 who commit offences or are in need of care & protection.

2   Comhairle (now called The Citizens Information Board) has responsibility for supporting the provision of information, advice and advocacy on a wide range of social and civil services in Ireland. Relevant legal and policy mandates are the Citizens Information Act 2007 and the Comhairle Act 2000; the Board comes under the remit of the Department of Social and Family Affairs.

3   As set out in the Mental Capacity Act 2005.

# 5 Forms of advocacy

> I learned that I could do everything that she (advocate) did if I knew all the information . . . that there are people who are genuinely there for you and can help to influence . . . I definitely got more self confident and learned to be assertive, how to communicate and how to get things that you want.
>
> (Young woman aged 25, in Chase et al. 2006: 60)

Within the provision of advocacy for various user groups in different situations, a number of forms of advocacy have been developed to safeguard people and support them to come to voice in particular settings and contexts. The development of many of these are primarily rooted in the democratic model of participation outlined in Chapter 3, as service user movements have campaigned to have more control over their lives and influence in the provision and delivery of services that impact on them. What is clear is that there is no single form of advocacy. However, forms of advocacy overlap and children and young people may require support in various ways depending on their reason for working with an advocate. Table 5.1 summarizes the main forms that we will examine in this chapter. Each form will be examined and the commonalities and differences will be discussed.

## Self-advocacy

> For me it means that I can speak for myself. It means I've got a voice and even without a voice I can communicate in other ways. It means yes and no – most important – 'No, I don't want tea, I want coffee, I didn't want sugar' – all the things we take for granted. It means people must listen to me, I can take a risk, I can have a relationship, that can be hard. I can think for myself, I can go to the shop with support and if I need help people can help me. I can cry if I want to cry. Take

**Table 5.1** Forms of advocacy

|  | Form of advocacy | Key characteristics | Model |
|---|---|---|---|
| Do-it-yourself advocacy | Self-advocacy | Young person expresses own feelings. Individual or group | Individual issue-based advocacy |
|  | Collective advocacy | Group of young people in a similar situation | Usually cause/systemic advocacy |
| Outsider advocacy | Citizen advocacy | A long-term relationship between a young person and their advocate | Individual covering any situation where a young person may need support |
|  | Peer advocacy | Advocate has had similar experiences for the young person being supported. Individual or group | Individual and often issue-based. Can also be collective systemic advocacy |
|  | Professional advocacy | Advocate trained and paid | Usually short-term and issue-based advocacy |
|  | Non-directed advocacy | Advocate supports people whose form of communication is difficult to interpret or who lack capacity | Individual issue-based advocacy |
|  | Legal advocacy | A contractual (and financial) relationship between advocate and person being represented | Individual issue-based advocacy |
|  | E-advocacy |  | Individual issue-based or systemic advocacy |

responsibility and make myself responsible. It means other things to other people.

(Jackie, in Goodley 2000: 81)

This is a form of advocacy that many people use every day (Brandon 1995) and quite simply involves speaking out or standing up for one's rights as a person (Goodley 2000). However, children and young people living away from home presenting as confident self-advocates may also be perceived to be demanding. Much of the literature about self-advocacy relates to adults who have learning difficulties and self-advocacy has been described as challenging the identity they have been assigned (Brandon 1995). More broadly, the term has been used to represent the self-determination of minority groups (particularly those with learning difficulties) and members of the group are therefore known as self-advocates. For individuals, this is about having the confidence and ability to express one's own feelings, to make choices and to influence decisions in relation to health, education, work and daily living (Simons 1998; Goodley 2000). For people using services, such decisions may often be taken in formal contexts as part of individual programme plans or, for children and young people in particular, in decision-making fora such as review meetings[1], family group conferences[2], case conferences or education planning meetings. However, some looked after children's and young people's experiences of self-advocacy in, for example, review meetings, have left them feeling their involvement was tokenistic, and that they were being judged by others attending the meeting (Boylan 2005; Boylan and Ing 2005).

For some young people in transition, developing self-advocacy skills through working with a group of young people in a similar position or using self-advocacy tools to explore some of the questions that they need to consider is helpful in enabling them to participate in the decision making at this important stage in their lives (Box 5.1).

In the UK, the beginnings of self-advocacy are generally located with the appearance in 1984 of the organization People First, although people with learning difficulties in long-stay institutions have tried to stand up for themselves for many years (Buchanan and Walmsley 2006; Traustadottir 2006) (see Box 5.2). Its development has been rather ad hoc, with a number of diverse activities becoming identified under the self-advocacy umbrella (Buchanan

---

**Box 5.1**   Asist transition project

Asist, an established advocacy charity for adults, secured funding in 2002 to help young people in transition. The project is based in North Staffordshire and supports one transition advocate and two part-time peer advocates. The transition project supports four special schools with self-advocacy projects that meet fortnightly. The groups have a specific aim to explore transition and the choices that young people have to make as they move into adulthood. Each member of the group is given a folder entitled 'All about me'. This folder is a self-advocacy tool that is used as the basis of the group meetings. The subjects that the group covers include 'who they are', 'who and what they like' and 'what they might want to do after school'. As the group has developed, the members have taken on ownership of the meetings – moving from just getting out the chairs to identifying a list of jobs that members can volunteer to do, deciding what subjects should be discussed and how meetings should be conducted. Notes from the meetings form part of a newsletter about the four self-advocacy groups, which is distributed to all special schools to share information.

---

**Box 5.2**   Tom's story

*The staff in the apartment encourage us to speak up about what we want. I think that is good but it is difficult. In the institution I was punished when I spoke up and I kept thinking that my demands would lead to conflict and punishment. I do not like conflict and punishment.*

(Tom Allen, in Traustadottir 2006: 177)

Tom Allen was born in 1912 in New York. His story starts before 'self-advocacy' was recognized as a way of enabling people with learning difficulties to come to voice. During the first 45 years of his life in an institution there was only one clear example of what we now know as self-advocacy, which was when he stated that he wanted to move nearer to his old home town. His brother and sister were invited to a meeting and with their support he was allowed to move. This first act of speaking up took place in the 1970s when both residents and staff were beginning to recognize that Tom and other residents had rights as citizens to a voice in their own lives. Once he had moved he was able to develop his self-advocacy skills, asking for a motorized wheelchair, and to be moved to another building. With the help of his brother and encouragement from my friends among the staff he was able to ask to be moved to a group home and at the age of 69 in 1982, when self-advocacy was becoming recognized in the US, he moved to another institution from which he hoped he would be able to move into the community. There he joined a self-advocacy group which helped him to become more assertive and advocate for his wish to move into his own home. Unfortunately his brother would not support him in this, believing that Tom was too old and frail to move. Without his brother's consent he could not move out. However he joined a group of other residents who filed a law suit against the state of New York to release them from the institution into the community. Eventually Tom moved into an apartment and had a personal assistant who helped him to speak up about his wishes and the things he wanted do on a daily basis: 'We read the paper in the morning and when the weather is good we go out. We go downtown, go shopping, visit different places and have lunch in a restaurant. In the summer we go to the beach, for a picnic or boat rides on the Finger Lakes. Lisa also helps me go fishing which I like very much'.

(Adapted from Traustadottir 2006: 178)

---

and Walmsley 2006). Primarily for individuals, this has focused on helping people to develop a sense of identity.

In a study examining the self-advocacy of people who have learning difficulties, Goodley and Armstrong explore the impact of advocacy on their lives and suggest that:

> Crucial to emergent understandings of self-advocacy is to note that it is a phenomenon created in direct relationship to a variety of (lacking) opportunities and chances. It does *not* just emerge as a direct consequence of self-advocacy group membership but often has wider familial, cultural, social and historical origins. This illuminates what Corker (2001) means by the centrality of life experiences to any understanding of disability politics and identity: self-advocacy is not something that can be artificially pinned onto those who need it but something organically and culturally created by enabling and, paradoxically, disabling environments.
>
> (Goodley and Armstrong 2001: 8)

Goodley and Armstrong develop a theoretical understanding of the concept by listening to narratives of people involved with self-advocacy and suggest that it occurs both inside and outside of what has been identified as the self-advocacy movement. This movement is a social movement, where groups of people voice common concerns or lobby for change in policy and practice (Brandon 1995; Atkinson 1999; Goodley 2000). The self-advocacy movement is one part of the broader disability rights/independent living movement and has also been described as a 'civil rights movement', since it is fundamentally concerned with improving the civil rights of people who have been and still are oppressed, and excluded because of how they are viewed as people who have or are labelled as having learning difficulties (Williams and Schoultz 1982). The history of the movement is difficult to trace but in the late 1960s a group of people with learning difficulties compiled a list of requests about how they felt services should be provided, which they then gave to the parent organization supporting them. While the outcome of this action is unknown, Goodley (2000: 9) notes that 'something unprecedented and previously undocumented had occurred'[3].

Buchanan and Walmsley (2006) state that these two elements of this form of advocacy – individual and collective – have led to competing constructions of self-advocacy, noting that the 'two do not sit easily together' (p. 134). Individuals using self-advocacy groups as a way of becoming confident and skilled in speaking up need to be part of a group with an ongoing programme of inducting and supporting new people. On the other hand, self-advocacy groups that are campaigning for change need to be more established with members who have the experience and sophisticated skills necessary for activism. They argue that the individual approaches to self-advocacy that have developed over the last two decades, focusing on acquiring skills and recording life stories, do not address the wider political context and sources of oppression. The campaigning element therefore operates in a climate where some people on behalf of whom campaigns are being fought are unaware of the political factors that impact on their lives. There are clearly issues, there-fore, about representation in respect of the campaigning elements of the movement. Nevertheless, the campaigning arguably has been successful, as recognition that people with learning difficulties have a right to a 'voice' is now reflected in legislation in England in the white paper *Valuing People* (Department of Health 2001). However, the danger of assimilation into ser-vice structures is only too apparent here, with self-advocacy developing as another contracted service trying to meet imposed targets (Buchanan and Walmsley 2006) and losing the ability to support individuals.

## Collective advocacy

> The minibuses were sprayed a standard colour with Social Services written across the side. We felt embarrassed to be seen in them and felt that it was another way of stigmatising us as children and young people in care. After years of talking the department agreed not to spray any new buses and not to have Social Services across the side.
>
> (Patel 1995: 10)

Although self-advocacy may be undertaken by a person individually or in a group, with a mutually inclusive relationship between the two (Goodley 2000), the collective aspect to self-advocacy outlined in the previous section has also developed in several ways and a typology of advocacy groups has emerged, which indicates further differences within advocacy practice (Goodley 2000). Four models of self-advocacy groups have been identified that reflect the structure of various groups and their relationship with others such as parents or professionals: the 'autonomous' or 'ideal' model, the 'divisional' model, the 'coalition' model and the 'service system' model (Box 5.3).

A connection can be made between the 'service-system' model and advo-cacy services for children and young people in receipt of welfare services. Where advocacy is commissioned by a local authority – with a service level agreement – the advocacy service is effectively within the service delivery sys-tem, whatever attempts are made to create independence from it[4]. There is a paradox here: although it is important to actively encourage such groups within services, the danger is that, as we have seen with self-advocacy groups for adults with learning difficulties above, once established they become inte-grated into the system and part of the bureaucracy they are set up to challenge (Goodley 2000; Payne 2000a; Clarke 2003). While these models are helpful in identifying the range of ways that groups of people are enabled to advocate for themselves there are problems in imposing such rigid classifications, since

| **Box 5.3**   Models of collective advocacy | | | |
|---|---|---|---|
| *Model* | *Example* | *Advantages* | *Problems* |
| Autonomous model | People First[5] | Seen as the most empowering. Groups in this model include:<br>• operate independently<br>• promote peer support through regular meetings<br>• are supported by non-disabled advisors | |
| Divisional model | Origins of this model are in existing parent or professional organizations (e.g. Scope[6], MENCAP[7]) | • There are advisors who may be trained advocates<br>• Provides access to the resources of the parent organization | Can create potential for conflicts of interest between the self-advocates and parents or professionals<br>Parent organizations have the power to control the advocacy group – if its concerns take precedence, the group becomes tokenistic |
| Coalition model | West of England Coalition for Independent Living[8] | • Coalition increases their political power<br>• Advisors can be both trained and disabled themselves | It may favour articulate and politically motivated members and thus marginalize others |
| Service system model | User groups within a residential setting, or a committee at a day centre | Groups are located within a service delivery system | Criticized most vociferously as being tokenistic, as group members can find it difficult to challenge the system that has set it up |

many groups do not fit neatly into the categories outlined. Furthermore, the negativity of labelling groups as more or less empowering means that 'the political ambitions, aims and actions of supporters and, more importantly, self-advocates go unrecognised, hidden behind a negative label' (Goodley 2000: 23).

There is a history of collective advocacy for children and young people pioneered by children and young people looked after in public care. These children and young people are, by definition, likely to need advocacy support 'because they are without their natural advocates, their parents' (Herbert and Mould 1992: 121). Historically, looked after young people's experiences have been ignored or their views sought via an adult informant. Consequently, they have lacked a single interest voice and have been denied the opportunity to self-organize or act on their own behalf (Frost and Stein 1989). However, the establishment of the National Association of Young People In Care (NAYPIC) in 1979 – a group for children and young people looked after in local authority care – provided a collective challenge to this trend.

One of the distinguishing features of NAYPIC was its commitment to the principle of self-organization and a constitution that restricted adult involvement.[9] NAYPIC played a key role in revealing and challenging poor practice in residential care and investigated allegations of the abuse of looked after young people. Subsequently, it submitted evidence to a range of inquiries into the abuse of children in residential care and the Wagner Working Group on Residential Care (NAYPIC 1983).

Subsequent 'in-care' groups have built on the success of NAYPIC and the establishment and influence of these groups as an expression of both self- and collective advocacy is well documented (Patel 1995; Boylan and Boylan 1998;

---

**Box 5.4** Aims of NAYPIC

NAYPIC (with the help of independent adult advisors) had the following aims:

- To promote the views and opinions of young people in care and those who have left care
- To offer advice and assistance to young people in care and ex-care
- To educate the public and childcare professionals on matters relating to young people in care and those who have left care.

It concentrated its efforts and successfully campaigned on 4 main issues:

- Influencing national child care policy
- Carrying out surveys on key issues relating to young people's care experiences
- Developing links with Social Services Departments
- Supporting the development of local groups

(Frost 1999: 118)

Lindsay 1998). Such groups provide a forum for both the individual and collective voices of looked after children – to inform, reflect on, endorse and challenge child care policy and practice at a national level. They may also enable and facilitate the development and consolidation of young people's self-advocacy. However, 'there is a danger that without appropriate support, self-advocacy groups can be set up to fail' (Dalrymple and Hough 1995: 4). From the perspective of young people, the role of adult involvement in self-advocacy groups should be determined by the young people concerned and may be restricted to the initial stages of setting up the group, being available thereafter in an advisory capacity (Patel 1995).

The role of advisors in relation to self-advocacy has not been embraced uncritically. In his exploration of relationships between advisors and self-advocates, Goodley (2000) discusses the complexities of advisor support. He uses Lukes's (1974) analysis of power to argue that there is a potential for advisors to unconsciously disempower, as in the ways that they address, talk and act with children and young people. While Goodley examines self-advocacy in the lives of people who have a learning disability, it does indicate that the role of an adult advisor should be rooted in the promotion of young people's tangible and meaningful self-determination and self-advocacy. Arguably, commitment to a strengths approach is key here with an understanding of how discourses of childhood and youth inform attitudes to children and young people. Advisors who support well are those who listen and act to challenge the discourses that silence and oppress.

The publication of *People Like Us* (Utting 1997) endorses and calls for the promotion of collective advocacy for 'in-care groups,' run for and by young people who are themselves in the care system. Utting (1997) envisaged that young people in local authority care should have a central role in informing the development of policy and practice. He suggested that this could be achieved through both the provision of children's rights and advocacy services and the development of self- and collective advocacy groups modelled on NAYPIC and Voices from Care[10]. In-care groups provide a forum for looked after children and young people to receive knowledge and information about their rights, share the range of their experiences and concerns of being in care, and support each other over particular issues. For Patel (1995: 7), in-care groups provide 'a collective voice which is a powerful tool for change'.

## Citizen advocacy

> We are genuinely good friends. Sometimes we can talk through difficult things – other times we just muck about. Even though we have been through some tough, difficult times over the past year there's always been positive sides. I am really pleasantly surprised at how

close we are. I never expected that – I thought it would be a more formal role, just representing someone at meetings.

(Sounds Good Project 2005: 23)

Citizen advocacy developed to support people who are unable to advocate for themselves or who require specific support to advocate for themselves. The concept of citizen advocacy emerged in the 1950s, although it did not begin to establish itself until the late 1960s. Since then, the ideology underpinning citizen advocacy has been severely criticized because of its identification of advocates as 'valued' citizens (Atkinson 1999). There is an assumption here that the partner is *not* a valued person, which colludes with discriminatory societal views of disabled people and begs the question about who is a 'valued' citizen. More recent definitions state that 'citizen advocacy is about individual active citizenship, where an ordinary member of the community makes a commitment to the rights of another who is disadvantaged and/or socially excluded' and as such has been described as 'informal facilitative advocacy' (CAIT 2002: 1), which is 'different from but complimentary to other forms of advocacy' (CAIT 2002: 2).

Citizen advocacy has primarily developed to support adults, but for young people with learning difficulties linking to an advocate in an informal relationship can give them the support they require over time to enable them to communicate their views and gain more control over their lives. There are a few projects that specifically recruit young volunteers to work with young people. This is different to many advocacy projects that traditionally recruit advocates who are older. Clearly, though, a young person is more likely to talk with someone their own age than 'someone who thinks like my Mum thinks' (Sounds Good Project 2005: 16). While this may be difficult for both parents and professionals, we can see from the case example in Box 5.5 that a relationship that is outside the control of both professionals and adults has the potential to be useful (Harnett 2003).

Underpinned by the consumerist approach to participation, citizen advocacy essentially involves a one-to-one relationship between a volunteer advocate and an individual like Kaye (Box 5.5) who is vulnerable and at risk of exclusion and who will therefore find it difficult to challenge professional systems (Smith and Ing 1996). The characteristics of citizen advocacy are:

- The citizen advocate defends their partner's rights as a citizen.
- The independence of the advocate is regarded as a crucial element, although it is an interdependent relationship in terms of the two people involved (Brandon 1995; Atkinson 1999).
- A citizen advocate has been described as someone who 'may become as a friend, helping their advocacy partner develop the skills needed

---

**Box 5.5** Emma and Kaye

---

Emma aged 17 is a trendy and lively, physical disabled young person, who is quite able to say what she wants. Kaye is equally trendy and lively with a warm personality. She is 19 and works as a hairdresser. Emma was finding it difficult and stressful to cope with the decision-making processes associated with leaving school and the many meetings that were taking place as the time was coming for her to leave. She felt caught between what the school thought was best for her and what her mother thought was best. Emma spent the summer feeling tense as she tried to mull things over and think about the opinions and advice from everyone involved in her care.

At first she was not keen on the idea of an advocate. However, she did agree to meet a potential advocate after the summer holidays – providing that her mother could go with her and stay with her if that was what she wanted. They arranged to meet in a pub and as soon as Emma met Kaye she became interested – here was someone her own age who seemed friendly and wanted to spend time with her in a pub! After half an hour Emma asked her mother to go and pick her up later.

Emma and Kaye talked for an hour about all kinds of things they were both interested in – men, going out, music, etc. Emma also confided to Kaye that she had an important meeting the following day that she was quite nervous about. She told Kaye what she wanted to do when she left school. After 18 months the two were close. Because of her physical disability Emma used to have her hair done at home – now she goes to Kaye's trendy salon and has her hair done in up-to-date styles. They still go out to the local pub together and Kaye's family support the relationship.

There is no ending to this story – Kaye is definitely still there for Emma and Emma can turn to Kaye whenever she needs to.

(Adapted from Sounds Good Project 2005: 50)

---

to get the most out of life and helping them gain acceptance into the life of the community' (KLDA 2002)[11].

- Citizen advocacy can widen the social networks of a partner (Atkinson 1999).
- Advocates may provide practical help and assistance (Simons 1993).
- It is less crisis orientated or issue based.
- For those whose everyday lives are often in the hands of service providers, it ensures that their everyday needs, preferences and wishes are taken into account (Ramcharan 1995). It includes helping people to access complaints systems.

There have been many changes in the way that citizen advocates work over the last 50 years. This can be seen in the comment from an advocacy coordinator in Box 5.6, which indicates both that young people who require advocacy support may be matched with someone their own age but also that the advocacy task for citizen advocates is becoming more complex. For example, working with social work managers to challenge health care provision for young disabled people in further education is both a time-consuming and a skilled task. Acknowledgement that advocacy can transform the lives of people with learning disabilities (Department of Health 2001) has been heralded as validating citizen and self-advocacy. This brings with it the suggestion that this form of advocacy is at the crossroads of its development. The traditional concept of citizen advocacy as being an individual form of case advocacy is being challenged, as it is now presented with the opportunity to contribute to policy that is also empowering (Eustace 2002).

---

**Box 5.6**  Working with young volunteers

Some advocates are writing to and meeting social work managers because current provision in day centres and college does not provide adequate health care for some partners who have complex disabilities and medical needs. The introduction of young advocates into these scenarios can be challenging for professionals. It can be hard for them to view a young non-professional as capable of being an advocate. The philosophy of recruiting young non-professional advocates can be very empowering for the young disabled person, but does go against our society's culture of professionalising and accrediting. Initially we had our own reservations about a young person's capability of taking on some of the issues. However we have found that young people are capable. They are passionate about people's rights. The challenge is for people to start listening. Currently I view this as an area where intensive support is put in from me – both in preparing the advocate and in preparing the professionals to respect the young person.

(Dunfermline Advocacy Coordinator, in Sounds Good Project 2005: 18)

---

## Peer advocacy

Peer advocacy occurs when the advocate shares similar circumstances with the person they are working with, for example they may also be using services or have had experience as a service user. In principle, peer advocacy can be based on citizen advocacy or self-advocacy with the distinction that the basis of peer advocacy is that shared experiences facilitate a relationship through mutual understanding. For some, peer advocates may be more acceptable than other people because of that common understanding (Atkinson 1999). This is supported by research indicating that where advocates can draw on their personal experiences, the relationship is likely to be productive (Boylan 2008). This form of advocacy also involves a partnership approach, although it is a less formalized way of working with a value base more aligned to self-advocacy than to citizen advocacy. While peer advocacy may also be similar to other forms of peer support such as mentoring for example, the difference is that peer advocacy is concerned with 'representing young people's views with the intention of influencing change' (Harnett 2004: 1).

For children and young people, most peer advocacy seems to be group based. Using the collective form of advocacy, children and young people are brought together to develop skills either to advocate for themselves or on behalf of the group. There are fewer examples of one-to-one peer advocacy, mainly supporting young disabled people[12].

Peer advocacy is not easy however, and a report examining models of peer advocacy identified a number of themes, highlighting the difficulties of peer advocacy (Harnett 2004). Problems included:

- The process of recruitment – not only can this be time consuming but also young people feel stigmatized by being identified with certain groups.
- Maintaining stable group membership – membership can constantly change, often because of the transient and chaotic lifestyle of young people who require advocacy support, which inevitably disrupts the progress of a group.
- Creating a supportive environment is necessary for a group to run successfully but is also time consuming.
- Managing the tension between providing individual support for young people in need and working towards specific objectives.
- Keeping young people motivated.
- Running peer advocacy groups – this is a skilled task.
- Getting young people's voices heard – the difficulty of engaging with service providers and professionals can be a real barrier to effective peer advocacy (Harding 1995, cited in Harnett 2004). Brandon (1995: 120) points out that a peer advocate can be made to feel 'unqualified to question or deal with "the professionals" ' with 'little credibility with the workers, and . . . very much alone' (Brandon 1995: 120).

Nevertheless, there are successful examples of peer advocacy, one of the most notable being Voices from Care in Wales. Drawing on nearly 20 years of experience, Voices from Care has ensured that the Welsh Assembly

Government's inquiry into the commissioning of advocacy services recognizes that peer advocacy and self-advocacy are 'critical elements' (Children and Young People Committee 2008) of a national advocacy strategy. Consequently, Recommendation 5 of the report states that:

> The Welsh Assembly Government should ensure that the advocacy unit provides training for local advocacy services, to assist them in coaching children and young people, using their services, to 'self advocate' and 'peer advocate' in the future.
>
> (Children and Young People Committee 2008: 15)

## Professional advocacy

> she gave me some power back . . . all the others, teachers, social workers etc were talking amongst themselves but no one was talking to me, they were not involving me or explaining anything to me.
>
> (Chase et al. 2006: 36)

At the other end of the spectrum, professional advocacy has developed partly because of the diminishing advocacy role undertaken by health and social services personnel (Simons 1993; Ivers 1998; Dalrymple 2004b; Boylan and Braye 2006) and partly because of the difficulties services users face in communicating with one or more powerful professionals. This has occurred in particular in services for children and young people (Ivers 1998; Payne 2000a) where most advocacy services employ paid advocates (Oliver et al. 2005; Pithouse et al. 2005). Describing advocates as 'professionals' is promulgated by those involved with advocacy services themselves. A publication by the Children's Rights Officers and Advocates organization describes advocates as a 'new breed of professionals' (Willow and Barry 1998). When the first national advocacy service, ASC, was established in England, there was a very clear attempt made to establish a professional profile on the grounds that this would be most advantageous for children and young people who were challenging services dominated by professional adults (Dalrymple and Payne 1995). Since then, legislative mandates for advocacy have had an impact on the development of this form of advocacy.

Professional advocacy has been described as the key characteristic of Specialist Independent Mental Health Advocacy (IMHA) Services for people subject to the powers of mental health legislation[12]. Volunteers are not expected to undertake the IMHA role as they have to be trained and supervised. As with citizen advocacy, this specific issue-based advocacy is seen as complementary to other advocacy provision. Similar forms of advocacy are expected to be provided for young people making a complaint under the

Children Act 1989 (Adoption and Children Act 2004) and Independent Complaints Advocacy Services (ICAS) within the National Health Service. Furthermore, the standards for advocacy services (Department of Health 2002; Welsh Assembly Government 2003) clearly shape advocacy practice. While these standards are not intended to be prescriptive, being described as a starting point to 'establish a framework for best practice' (Department of Health 1999: 6), they do indicate the need for professional approaches through the provision of quality services. Recognition of the professional role of independent advocates is also recognized in the proposed framework for advocacy in Wales that suggests that all advocates working with children and young people will be registered with the Care Council for Wales with training (and qualification) being linked to registration requirements. As we can see from the example in Box 5.7, the need for advocates to be able to deal with formal and difficult situations demands knowledge and expertise such as that offered by professional advocates.

There are also a number of specific professional positions that identify professional advocacy within their work. In particular, the development of Children's Rights Officers has been important in establishing professional advocacy in work with children and young people. In 1987, Mike Lindsay was appointed the first Children's Rights Officer in Britain, to support and promote the rights of young people 'looked after' by the local authority. We saw in Chapter 1 that his work had two main strands:

- A children's rights service to inform children and staff about what rights they should have if they were looked after by the local authority in Leicester; and importantly
- To take up specific issues on behalf of individual children and young people

(James 1992)

Lindsay set out to ensure that he brought a 'professional approach' to children's rights (Lindsay 1998: 5) and he was a supporter of the establishment of CROA (Children's Rights Officers and Advocates) in 1992 as a membership organization to represent the professional interests of children's rights officers and advocates. The organization now provides a forum for professionals engaged in children's rights; promotes the development of children's rights and advocacy services; and informs practice development through the dissemination of research in the field of children's rights.

More broadly, Commissioners for Children's Rights are identified as professional advocates. An advocacy theme can be seen in the aims outlined by the European network of Ombudsmen in Box 5.8, and we saw in Chapter 1 that the need for independent commissioners has been recognized by the four nations of the UK, despite the fact that they have varying mandates.

**Box 5.7**   Professional advocacy support for Ahmed

Ahmed is 14 and has been on a full care order since he was 10. He has had numerous placements within the local authority and a history of missing for considerable periods. As a result he was found an out of authority placement where he stayed for about 18 months. While there Ahmed sustained serious injuries to his face and eye during an incident involving an older young man. Soon after he was returned to the local authority. Ahmed put in a claim for Criminal Injuries Compensation but because of many changes of social worker and periods when he had no social worker allocated, the claim was ongoing for several years. He finds continually going into the details of the incident distressing. Unfortunately he has become disillusioned with Social Services, which does not always help his cause and has resulted in a reputation for being a difficult young person. He refused to meet a newly allocated (sixth) social worker on the basis that she would leave in a couple of months. With the deadline for the Criminal Injuries Claim getting close he was helped by a residential social worker to access the advocacy service so that he could progress his claim. Together they worked to progress the claim and develop a relationship with Ahmed's new social worker.

(Adapted from evidence presented to the Children, Schools and Families Committee by Voice and The Children's Society on behalf of the Advocacy Consortium 2008)

**Box 5.8**   Aims of Children's Commissioners

- To promote full implementation of the UNCRC;
- To promote a higher priority for children in central, regional or local government and in civil society, and to improve public attitudes to children;
- To influence law, policy and practice, both by responding to governmental and other proposals and by actively proposing changes;
- To promote effective co-ordination of government for children at all levels;
- To promote effective use of resources for children;
- To provide a channel for children's views and to encourage government and the public to give proper respect to children's views;
- To collect and publish data on the situation of children and/or encourage the government to collect and publish adequate data.

(European Network of Ombudsmen for Children at www.ombudnet.org)

Commissioners throughout the world use the UNCRC as the framework to underpin their work and have achieved a great deal for children and young people, including promoting reforms in law, advocating the views of children and young people, highlighting discrimination of vulnerable groups, and increasing knowledge and understanding about children's rights (Children's Rights Alliance for England 2003). The European network of Ombudspeople for Children publishes annual assessments of the work of twenty institutions, showing that the appointment of Commissioners clearly creates a climate of respect for children and young people, which in turn enhances their status and enables them to come to voice. While they exist in different legal structures and have varying roles, Commissioners are generally able to influence government policy and have an awareness-raising function.

## Non-instructed advocacy

More recently, a form of advocacy that has gained increasing recognition is non-directed or non-instructed advocacy. This first became part of the advocacy agenda within adult services with people who lack capacity or have dementia. The rationale underpinning this form of advocacy is that there are people whose method of communication is difficult to interpret or who lack capacity, who have the right to have their likely views and preferences considered by decision makers. As the name suggests, in this form of advocacy the child or young person has not expressed a view that needs to be listened to. Rather, non-instructed advocacy involves an advocate responding to a request from a key person in the life of the child or young person and assessing what their views or choices might be. The issue of non-directed advocacy is one that is being debated both in relation to advocacy services for children and young people and within adult advocacy services. In the latter, the concept appears to be one that is becoming accepted as a form of advocacy practice. The Mental Capacity Act 2005 provides a statutory framework for independent mental capacity advocates to safeguard vulnerable people who lack capacity in specific situations[13] and has brought debates about non-directed advocacy into sharp focus.

The term 'non-instructed' or 'non-directed' is challenging in terms of thinking about the advocacy role. The definitions of advocacy explored in Chapter 4 identify the key elements as supporting and enabling people to say what they want; empowering people to be involved in decisions concerning their lives; and working in partnership to ensure that *their* wishes and views are represented rather than those of the advocate or any other interested party. This means that any models devised to support people who cannot instruct an advocate are problematic. It is therefore helpful to examine the four approaches to non-instructed advocacy that have emerged:

### A 'person-centred' approach

This approach is underpinned by the key advocacy principle that given time, resources and a specialist advocate with the relevant skills, most young people *can* communicate their wishes and feelings. It means that the advocate has to develop a relationship of trust with the young person, and build up a picture of what life is like for them. This enables them to then suggest what the young person's preferences are (Lawton 2006). However, Mercer (2008) points out that the danger here is that advocates may make statements based on their own bias and need to be able to evidence the claims they make to demonstrate their neutrality as an advocate.

### A 'human rights' approach

All advocacy services for young people are underpinned by the United Nations Convention on the Rights of the Child. In this approach, the advocate uses the law to ensure that any actions taken by decision makers uphold and promote the rights of the young person. The advocate looks at available options on the basis of the rights of the person concerned, which may be a different perspective to other professionals whose judgements may be based on prevention of risk, maintenance of health, care principles or 'best interests'[14]. Here, therefore, the advocate makes a judgement based on a consideration of the rights of the young person involved. Box 5.9 overleaf indicates how advocates taking this approach might come to that judgement. The issue for advocates here is the need to take care that, by concentrating on rights, the opportunity to find out about the individual is not missed (Mercer 2008). Furthermore, such independent scrutiny may well be valid but does not really equate to advocacy.

### A 'watching brief' approach

This is a particular approach developed by Asist, an advocacy service based in Staffordshire, as a way of working with people who cannot communicate in a way that the advocate is able to recognize. This approach tests any proposal against 'eight domains to a quality life':

- Competence
- Community presence
- Continuity
- Choice and influence
- Individuality
- Status and respect
- Partnerships and relationships
- Well-being

(Asist 2006, cited in Mercer 2008)

---

**Box 5.9**   Questions an advocate could ask when pursuing a rights-based approach

- Have the decision makers taken every effort to ascertain the wishes and feelings of the young person?
- How have these been taken into account?
- How have the opinions of carers, friends and professionals regarding the young person's wishes and feelings been taken into account?
- Has the advocate had adequate time to formulate a relationship and understand preferred communication methods?
- Has the young person been invited to the meeting?
- What efforts have been made to ensure the participation of the young person?
- What efforts have been made to present information in an appropriate manner?
- What needs have been identified?
- How are these being met?
- Are the young person's care plan, education plan and/or pathway plan up to date and current?
- Have contact arrangements been discussed and met?

(Reprinted with permission from Mercer 2008)

---

Box 5.10, opposite shows how the advocate might do this. The rationale here is that even though a vulnerable person may be unable to instruct an advocate, their human rights can be promoted by the advocate.

### A 'best interests' approach

We saw in Chapter 1 that professionals who have to take decisions in the 'best interests' of a child or young person invariably find it difficult to act also as an advocate. Clearly, a 'best interests' approach should be one that is taken by all professionals concerned with the care of a child or young person. Arguably, for an advocate to also take such an approach only adds to the range of views that may be presented and as such may do little more than muddy the waters.

This approach is perhaps the most controversial of the four. For children and young people, it conflicts with the first standard of the National Standards for the Provision of Children's Advocacy, which states that an advocate only acts with the express permission and instruction of the child or young person 'even when these are not the advocate's view of the child or young person's

---

**Box 5.10**    Questions an advocate could ask when using a watching brief approach

---

Advocates using a watching brief approach can ask questions that review the proposal against relevant domains, such as:

- How will the proposal promote the person's independence?
- How will the proposal manage risk?
- How will the proposal help the person maintain links with their past?
- How will the proposal involve the person in decision making?
- How will the proposal promote individuality?
- How will the proposal reduce prejudice and social stigma?
- How will the proposal provide opportunities for interaction with others?

(Taken from Asist 2006)

---

best interests' (Department of Health 2002; Welsh Assembly Government 2003). For some advocacy services, this is also an approach that they clearly avoid, as Box 5.11, overleaf shows.

The 'best interests' approach is also challenged by proponents of non-instructed advocacy, who put forward the human rights argument. They argue that a rights-based approach may well challenge professional views of the 'best interests' of a child or young person.

Most advocates who use non-instructed advocacy tend to use a combination of the four approaches. Non-instructed advocacy also works best when the advocate has a consistent 'eye' on taking instruction – so their approach is very fluid, using non-instructed advocacy and instructed advocacy interchangeably (for instance, a person who lacks capacity is unlikely to lack capacity permanently – there may be times when they can instruct). When working with children, it would mean advocates saying to themselves: 'I'm not clear what this eye movement means so I'll take the human rights approach now. But I'll also commit to learning what the eye movement means so that I can learn more about the communication style and therefore it will not be necessary to continue to rely on non-directed approaches' (Mercer 2008).

---

**Box 5.11** Xpress Advocacy Service, Hastings

---

Xpress, a well-established advocacy service in East Sussex, is very clear that it does not provide non-directed advocacy:

> *We believe that as advocates we work in partnership with the young people we support and this means that we do not take a 'best interest' view, but work alongside the young person. In all our work it is the young person who decides how to proceed in any situation. The role of the advocate is to make sure that the young person's view is heard and considered – even if the advocate disagrees with the young person.*

(Boylan and Dalrymple 2006: 28)

In situations where a young person is unable to instruct or direct the advocate, Xpress clearly states that it is not able to provide a service. However, the organization does work with young people who do not communicate verbally, finding that given time, resources and someone with the relevant skills to work with them, most young people can and do communicate their wishes and feelings. Xpress is committed to gaining the skills needed to communicate with children and young people who use different ways of expressing their viewpoint and believes that the central tenets of advocacy should not be compromised to accommodate their own lack of skills as advocates.

It is not always easy though to identify when what the organization is doing becomes non-directed advocacy. There have been situations when advocates have worked with a young person for a long time, but have been unable to demonstrate that they understood the role of the advocate. As an organization therefore Xpress recognizes the need to be able to assess when it is not able to provide advocacy support and refer on to another agency.

(Adapted from Boylan and Dalrymple 2006)

---

## Legal advocacy

Legal advocacy has a long established tradition, where the legal advocate represents the interests of the client, speaking on the client's behalf to protect their rights (Wertheimer 1996). Solicitors should be members of the children's panel of solicitors when representing looked after children and young people. King and Young acknowledge that there may be situations when the child's instructions are not seen to be in their best interests. The role of the solicitor is encapsulated as having:

A duty to counsel the child about the instructions but must not pressure the child to change instructions. If a competent child's instructions are ignored this can be damaging to the child. The child has the right for their instructions to be followed.

(King and Young 1992: 72)

For King and Young, the central importance should be the child's or young person's right to have their instructions presented to the court. They take the view that other social welfare practitioners will take a 'best interests' approach and that the child has the right for their view to be considered. King (1994) reflects on the limitations of the adversarial process in the UK, but at the same time argues forcefully that all children and young people should not be in a position where they are without legal representation. Legal advocacy is not without its shortcomings, however (Bateman 1995). The relationship is essentially of a contractual and financial nature and it is not equally accessible to all children and young people. However, there are a number of national organizations such as NYAS, Voice and the Children's Legal Centre that recognize the importance of ensuring that legal expertise is available to children and young people.

We can see from Box 5.12, overleaf how different forms of advocacy complement each other and that at different points in time a young person may need access to more than one form of advocacy support. 'A' was fortunate in that she lived in an area where there was access to a network of advocates. She first contacted an advocacy service for young people in public care. An advocate from this service was able to make A aware of her entitlements, dependent on her age. However, the service recognized the need for legal advocacy to support A through the complicated legal process required to enable her to legally establish her age. For young people like A, it is important that they have access to legal advocacy to determine age since this clearly has an impact on what the local authority is required to do by way of support. A needed support therefore to ensure that her voice was heard by the local authority and that her views and what she wanted were clear to the professionals involved in working with her. Without legal representation in this instance, it is unlikely that the local authority responsible for safeguarding the welfare of A would have discharged their statutory duties.

## Electronic advocacy

Electronic advocacy (also referred to as e-advocacy or net–activism) has empowering potential. It is a powerful mechanism for individual children and young people to log on, find out about advocacy through the net and make their initial contact electronically with an advocacy service. Young

---

**Box 5.12** Advocacy case study

---

The Children's Legal Centre is a unique, independent national charity concerned with law and policy affecting children and young people. It provides legal advice and representation to children, their carers and professionals throughout the United Kingdom. The Children's Legal Centre was contacted by an advocacy service for young people in public care following a referral from a school with a very concerning situation relating to one of their students.

On 1 December 2006, a young woman from Uganda arrived in the United Kingdom from the Democratic Republic of Congo. She arrived with a visa issued by the British Embassy in the DRC. This visa recorded her name as 'A' and her date of birth as 5 October 1992. The visa was issued for the purposes of reuniting A with her father, Mr B, who originated from Uganda and had been living in the United Kingdom for many years and was a British citizen.

Mr B and A had become estranged within 2 months of her entry into the UK. Mr B maintained that A was an elder daughter named 'C' who had stolen her younger sister's identity to enter the country. A denied this. There was no reliable documentation. Like thousands of other children entering the United Kingdom every year, A became a young person whose age was disputed and who was reliant on a Local Authority for support and protection.

It was important to define A's age as if A was a minor, the Local Authority had particular statutory obligations to provide for her welfare and needs. If she was an adult those obligations did not exist. The Local Authority argued that reports from A's carers indicated that some of her behaviour made her come across as an adult rather than a young person. They were dubious of her account of her life in Uganda and her flight out of the country. They examined A's demeanour and presentation and considered her to be significantly older than her stated age. A gave evidence, and confirmed her name and date of birth, having been told this information by her mother. She roundly denied being 'C' or being older. She cited the views of her teachers and other professionals involved in her care who viewed her as a minor to support her position.

A lived in a large urban centre with a comprehensive network of advocates in place for children and in particular those being looked after by Local Authorities. Through her advocate acting as litigation friend, A commenced legal proceedings to bar Mr B from returning her to Uganda against her will. She also challenged the accommodation being offered by the Local Authority as unsuitable given her stated age. The Local Authority had proposed to place A in semi-independent accommodation which would normally be allocated to children over 16. Access to an advocate ensured that A was aware of her entitlements and was adequately supported to pursue them.

A long and complicated legal process ensued to determine A's identity, age and by extension, the level of support owed to her by the Local Authority. Throughout this process, advocacy ensured that not only were A's legal interests protected but that her voice was heard.

English was not A's first language and although her spoken English was excellent, she often interpreted things in a more literal way than intended. Her advocate assisted in ensuring that A's views and preferences were clear to all those working with her.

Legal representation is critical in cases such as A's to ensure that local authorities discharge their statutory duties to safeguard the welfare of children.

(Case study kindly provided by the Children's Legal Centre)

people and advocates can communicate with each other via e-mail, text messages and other electronic resources. Electronic advocacy also facilitates communication between advocacy organizations across local, national and global dimensions, through online discussion or special interest groups. For advocates, therefore, electronic advocacy has a significant role to play in:

- providing information to particular groups of children and young people (such as those living away from home) about their rights and entitlements in the field of health, education and social work;
- the exchange of ideas and information between advocacy organizations;
- reducing the isolation of advocates who may operate in single worker posts;
- ensuring governments, policy makers and service providers are aware of children's and young people's perspectives;
- promoting collaborative practice and sharing of practice challenges (and solutions) across the advocacy community;
- enabling issue-based advocacy to inform systemic advocacy;
- promoting systemic change through mobilizing the advocacy community to respond to policy initiatives.

The development of electronic advocacy is relatively recent compared with other forms of advocacy. It is intended to complement rather than replace other forms. For example, if looked after children and young people use electronic advocacy to share information about what happens in the statutory reviews process or in a child protection case conference, it may help to reduce their sense of isolation and uncertainty. Having information may promote children's and young people's individual self advocacy, or provide information about other forms of advocacy support available to them (e.g. www.mazeadvocacy.net toolkit). Electronic advocacy also has the potential to extend the reach of collective advocacy for children and young people. Established and emerging 'in-care' groups can utilize the technology to exchange and disseminate issues and ideas with other groups of children and young people and in doing so build and extend collaborations.

## Summary

The changing context of policy has led to the rapid development of independent advocacy for children and young people as it has moved from the extraordinary to commonplace. It has become accepted practice in all four nations of the UK as the respective governments have started to promote the need for children and young people to have access to independent advocacy, and is now written into policy and legislation. This means that children and young people are entitled to an advocate in particular circumstances – notably when they are making a complaint. This can only be a positive move, bearing in mind the difficulties that children in the past have had when trying to complain about poor treatment (see Chapter 1). However, it does also mean that professional advocacy is the most developed form of advocacy support in relation to children and young people.

Consideration of the various forms of advocacy indicates that they can be divided into two broad groupings. 'Do-it-yourself' advocacy refers to cases where individual children or young people speak for themselves, or where a group of children and young people represent those in a similar position. 'Outsider advocacy' is where an individual child or young person or a group is supported or represented by someone (usually an independent adult advocate). It can be argued that the first type of advocacy emphasizes empowerment, even though there is usually a facilitator supporting the process, while the second type tends to emphasize the expertise or life skills of the external advocate (Weafer 2003).

Children and young people in receipt of services may at different times need access to particular advocacy support. However, although various forms of advocacy co-exist, there are clearly fundamental differences – different value bases and goals – which lead to both an interplay between them and confusion, despite the common goals of challenging oppressive systems and working towards empowerment and inclusion of children and young people (Brandon 1995; Smith and Ing 1996; Atkinson 1999). So, for example, citizen advocacy is based on the premise that a volunteer advocate, a citizen who is not contaminated by service perspectives, is best placed to support someone on a long-term basis, while for professional advocates it is important to know and understand the systems that are being challenged in order to promote the rights of children and young people within those systems, usually in relation to a particular issue.

For peer advocates, user-experience is the key factor and self-advocacy projects highlight the importance of service user empowerment. Similarly, various forms of collective advocacy may appear to be more or less empowering. However, the negativity of labelling groups in terms of empowerment means that 'the political ambitions, aims and actions of supporters and, more importantly, self-advocates go unrecognised, hidden behind a negative label' (Goodley 2000: 23). Furthermore, it is clear that in various ways user groups can provide 'safe environments' in which sometimes fragile identities can be supported, and confidence and skills can be developed (Barnes and Shardlow 1997).

The various forms of advocacy are also contested. For example, we saw in relation to the typologies outlined in relation to non-instructed advocacy that the notion of 'best-interests' advocacy contradicts advocacy principles. Therefore, although it is essential that specialist advocates are recruited and trained to work with young people who do not communicate verbally, advocates also need to be prepared to assess when advocacy is not possible. There will be occasions when someone other than an advocate may need to take action to safeguard against abuse. In addition, capacity can change over time, which in turn requires constant monitoring and re-assessment. The (adult) principles of the Mental Capacity Act 2005 are helpful in supporting this thinking, particularly that:

- individuals should be assumed to be capable of making their own decisions unless proved otherwise;
- everyone should be given the support they need to make their own decisions before they are judged incapable of doing so;
- people should be able to make 'eccentric' or unwise decisions – it is their capacity to make decisions not the decisions themselves that is the issue.

The issue of non-instructed advocacy, therefore, is clearly controversial. It remains essential that where young people are unable to instruct an advocate, they are not denied access to someone who can ensure, independently, that:

- they are safeguarded from abuse;
- services address all aspects of their care and treatment; and
- they are treated in the same way as someone who can instruct an advocate.

However, arguably this person should not be a professional/specialist advocate. Any professional working with young people should, as part of their role, be pro-actively safeguarding and promoting the rights and welfare of vulnerable young people. There remains a question then about whether what is currently referred to as 'non-instructed advocacy' is appropriately placed within the advocacy field or whether it is simply an extension of lobbying and campaigning arenas.

Professional advocacy is arguably the form that is provided by most advocacy services for children and young people. Its legitimation through various legislative mandates has provided the impetus and financial resources to enable advocacy services to be set up throughout the four nations of the UK. The problem here though is that resources become targeted at particular areas of advocacy practice and the provision of advocacy and who is entitled to an advocacy service becomes directed through legislation.

The theory and practice of the different forms of advocacy may appear to make it difficult to understand how these different and sometimes contradictory principles can work together. However, the changing, complex and sometimes chaotic lives of the children and young people who need advocacy support means that they need access to different forms of advocacy to ensure that their needs are met.

## Notes

1  Children and young people looked after in local authority care have regular statutory reviews.
2  Family group conferences are a family decision-making process.
3  See Goodley (2000) for a detailed account of the history of the movement.
4  Standard 6 of the National Standards (Welsh Assembly Government 2003) states that 'the advocacy service is, as far as possible, funded and managed in a way that ensures independence from the commissioning body, so that children and young people have confidence that their advocates will act for them and are free from any conflicts of interest' and that 'as far as possible, the service is not directly accountable to the management of any bodies exercising parental responsibility for the child or young person'.
5  People First  is a national organisation run by and for people with learning difficulties to raise awareness of and campaign for the rights of people with learning difficulties and to support self advocacy groups.
6  SCOPE is an organisation in England and Wales whose focus is people with cerebral palsy. Its aim is that disabled people achieve equality.
7  MENCAP is a charity that works with people who have a learning disability and their carers.
8  The West of England Centre for Inclusive Living (WECIL) was set up in 1995 and describes itself as an organization of disabled people working for disabled people. It provides a range of services to disabled people that enables them to live in the community and take control over their own lives, including a

Care Management Advocacy Project and a Disabled Mothers Advocacy Project.

9   NAYPIC's constitution laid down that adults could be involved in an advisory capacity only; it also restricted the involvement of over 25-year-old ex-care leavers.

10   An organization based in Wales run for and by young people in care, previously Welsh NAYPIC.

11   Kennet Advocacy Project for People with Learning Difficulties (KLDA) also identifies within its core principles that 'the relationship between the advocate and their partner is that of a professional working relationship' (KLDA 2002: 10), indicating that partners should not be led to believe that the relationship will be a continuing friendship.

12   Mental Health Act 2007; Mental Capacity Act 2005; Mental Health (Care and Treatment) (Scotland) Act 2003.

13   NHS bodies and local authorities have a duty to consult the independent advocate in decisions about serious medical treatment and changes of residence.

14   See the discussion paper arguing for non-directed advocacy by Rasbach et al. (2005).

# 6 Models for the provision of advocacy

## Introduction

Having considered the different forms of advocacy in Chapter 5, we now examine the development of models for the provision of advocacy services. Advocacy is a dynamic and evolving way of working, its profile having changed significantly during the course of the last fifteen years. This is reflected in the previous chapter, where we looked at forms of advocacy that operate within different contexts and with varying value bases. Furthermore, forms of advocacy such as self- and citizen advocacy are well established while non-instructed advocacy and e-advocacy are more recent. We therefore take the discussion further in this chapter to consider ways in which they operate within the context of services for children and young people. We begin with an examination of four models and consider how they enable us to understand the practice and provision of contemporary advocacy. We then present our own model, which aims to take into account aspects of the models outlined and also draws on models of participation from Chapter 3.

## Models of advocacy

### Issue-based and systemic model

> Advocacy projects need to remember the macro-level where policy is formulated rather than constantly evoking a 'band aid' approach. Individual advocacy cases should be fed upwards through lobbying and submissions to government so that structural change occurs at macro-level and fewer cases require advocacy.
>
> (Weafer 2003: 65)

We saw in Chapter 5 that some forms of advocacy relate to individuals (issue-based advocacy) while others have a collective focus. This has led to a model that recognizes the importance of both and their inter-dependence. Issue-based advocacy refers to work with individuals or small groups (e.g. families). Issue-based advocacy services are provided in two ways. Pro-active approaches involve routinely offering young people advocates in decision-making forums such as reviews, family group conferences, child protection conferences and representation and complaints procedures. This removes the responsibility from young people to contact an advocate themselves and gives them an opportunity to take up the offer of support if they need it. This method of providing advocacy is sometimes called *opt-out*, where the young person has to say that they do not want the advocacy service, rather than *opt-in*, where then the onus is on the young person to request advocacy support. Both methods can be criticized – arguably opt-out methods only work if children or young people feel able to say that they do not want or need an advocate, while opt-in methods only work if young people are aware that there is a service that they can access, which depends on how well it is marketed. Advocacy may also be pro-actively offered through regularly visiting children living away from home in residential units, boarding school or in young offender institutions. Pro-active advocacy therefore offers support to those young people who are unable to or unsure about referring themselves. Reactive services respond to requests from individual young people who identify the need for support with a specific issue.

Systemic advocacy refers to work with larger groups, usually aimed at  structural changes in relation to legislation, policy or practice. In their study of child advocacy groups in America, Richart and Bing (1989) set out some basic beliefs (taken from a study completed in 1983[1]) that underpin the work of advocates working with children and young people. Despite the fact that they are dated, these beliefs still stand in relation to the provision of advocacy in the UK today. They focus on the process of change and the reasons why children and young people might need advocacy support:

- Children and young people who are deemed to be at risk are consistently receiving poor quality services.
- These inequities may continue without the involvement of an advocate to argue for improved services for children and young people.
- Changes in policy have an important part to play in promoting needed improvements.
- Policy changes can only be implemented in ways that benefit children and young people if there is independent monitoring of the implementation process.

(Designs for Change 1983, cited in Richart and Bing 1989: 89)

From this we can see that advocacy has two important functions in promoting change. The first is to disturb the system concerned, for example aspects of health, education or welfare systems. The advocacy service UCAN[2] clearly recognized that advocacy goes beyond individual case work – it also involves influencing or 'disturbing' systems:

> Advocacy is a process for change, a process for learning. It stimulates respect for children's and young people's rights and promotes participation in the planning and challenging of the systems that impact on their lives. Acting on children's and young people's experiences and views, the advocacy extends beyond individual casework.
>
> (UCAN Annual Report 2004: 5)

The second is to apply pressure at a decision point necessary to make the systems more child and young person friendly – for example, when national governments are consulting on policy and legislative changes.

However, as in any practice that aims to promote change, advocacy at both the individual and systems levels are inevitably interrelated (Mickelson 1995) and a model for understanding advocacy links the two together. A relationship between issue-based and systemic advocacy is necessary, since

---

**Box 6.1**   Examples of National Government Consultations

The Welsh Assembly Government consulted on *A New Service Model for Delivering Advocacy Services to Children and Young People* (2007). Seventy organizations responded to this consultation, a large proportion of which were local and national advocacy services. http://new.wales.gov.uk/consultation/dhss/1853891/advocacy-responses-e. doc?lang=en

Voice and the Children's Society responded to the consultation by the Children, Schools and Families Committee on the Children's and Young Person's Bill (Lords) (House of Commons Children, Schools and Families Committee 2008).

The government consulted in England on Independent Mental Capacity Advocate (IMCA). Thirty-six independent advocacy organizations responded (Department of Health 2006a).

The government consulted on providing effective advocacy services for children and young people making a complaint under the Children Act 1989. Eight advocacy providers submitted a response (DfES 2004).

individual situations provide the data needed to promote change in legislation, systems and policies. Applying this model to child and youth advocacy, it can be seen that if children and young people are to have access to adequate and relevant services, be protected and have a voice in the decisions that affect their lives, all parts of the advocacy framework are needed. This means that, if advocacy is to make a difference, systemic advocacy is an important element of issue-based advocacy practice. The model shown in Box 6.2 was used to develop advocacy in Canada.

Over thirty years ago, advocacy for children and young people in America was described by Paul (1977) as 'a social movement directed to the rights of children', a description that fits well with the above framework. Richart and Bing (1989) also emphasize systemic advocacy as the primary goal of child advocacy organizations – to initiate change in the systems that impinge on the lives of children and young people. While the structure of such advocacy is different to those developing in the four nations of the UK and has been described as a 'beneficent and legalistic approach' (Boylan and Wylie 1999: 61) to advocacy, the model can usefully be used to inform advocacy elsewhere. Indeed, in many respects this model is similar to that suggested by the first Welsh Children's Commissioner (Clarke 2003), who, as we noted in Chapter 4, described three generic practices:

- issue-based advocacy (effectively issue-based advocacy in the model outlined above);

---

**Box 6.2** A Model for Understanding Advocacy

Root causes of many problems experienced by children and young people are systemic. Systemic change should support better issue-based solutions.

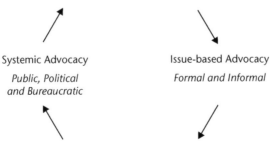

Systemic Advocacy
*Public, Political and Bureaucratic*

Issue-based Advocacy
*Formal and Informal*

Many issue-based situations cannot be resolved within the current system. Issue-based advocacy 'informs' our systemic advocacy and tells us what changes are needed.

(Preston 1997)

- relationship-based advocacy (effectively citizen advocacy as illustrated in the forms of advocacy but which could also fall into the issue-based advocacy category here); and
- general-issue advocacy (or systemic advocacy).

Clarke was clear that the same organization does not necessarily need to provide both issue-based and systemic advocacy. He indicated that it 'may be counter-productive for the same organisation to be engaged in providing both services' (Clarke 2003: 89). This is a debateable point, however, as both the model presented above and practice demonstrate. For example, Voices from Care Cymru specifically aims to create opportunities for all children and young people who are or have been looked after in Wales, to have an individual *and* collective voice at local and national levels so that their conditions and outcomes may be improved. Their approach includes campaigning (systemic advocacy) based on the experiences of young people (issue-based advocacy) as a specific element of its work:

> Voices from Care exists to improve conditions and outcomes for young people who are or have been looked after. The organisation actively campaigns around issues which are of concern to young people. We will work with other voluntary organisations, the media and through appropriate avenues in our campaign work.
> Voices from Care ensures that the views/experiences of young people who are or have been looked after are known at a policy-making and decision-making level. Where possible we try to ensure that young people are in direct dialogue with those responsible for shaping the care system.
>
> (www.vfcc.org.uk)

Another interesting example comes from an advocacy project based in Wales that worked with children and young people in child protection systems. From the experiences of children and young people and their advocates in child protection conferences, the project challenged the proceduralization of advocacy within this decision-making process and worked towards ensuring that a policy of child-centred practice was adopted by the local authority commissioning the service (Boylan and Wylie 1999; Wyllie 1999). Issue-based advocacy in this instance informed systemic advocacy, as the project worked 'not only to improve individual lives but also to contribute to policy and practice development … The emphasis on acting on children and young people's experiences has resulted in the project carrying out a range of work extending beyond individual advocacy' (Willow 2002: 77). Tros Gynnal, set up in 2002 to manage and develop children's rights, advocacy and participation work in Wales, was involved in issue-based advocacy through its membership of the Welsh Assembly Task and Finish Group[3]. In England, Voice for the Child in Care (VCC now called VOICE) clearly states the issue-based/systemic link in its annual review of 2001–2002:

> Using our experience of delivering advocacy and independent services and our work with children and young people as individuals and in groups around the country, VCC is in a unique position to campaign for changes in law, policy and practice on behalf of all children and young people in public care.
>
> (Voice for the Child in Care 2002: 10)

The National Youth Advocacy Service (NYAS) used information from its issue-based advocacy work in a publication for professionals (a quarterly publication entitled *Representing Children*) that emphasized the development of policy and practice. The Scottish Executive suggests that independent advocacy services should be a positive force for change, identifying some benefits of linking advocacy into the decision-making processes:

- They can link the experiences of their individual service users into common themes.
- They can provide feedback on users' perceptions of the way they are treated by different services, especially valuable where service users find it difficult to present this themselves.
- They can inform policy and practice in relation to future service provision.

> (Scottish Executive 2001)

### Passive and active model

Another way of thinking about advocacy has been identified by Hodgson (1995) (Box 6.3), overleaf. He suggests that there needs to be a continuum between what has been defined as passive and active advocacy. The two approaches relate to varying perspectives about children and young people either as individuals needing provision and protection or as citizens and active participants (Jenkins 1995). Passive advocacy involves the advocate speaking up for someone else (as in citizen advocacy, for example). For children and young people, Jenkins (1995) suggests that such an approach is mainly concerned with protecting children 'in terms of their entitlement to special status in, and consideration by, society' (p. 36). This links to protectionist perspectives on children's rights. Active advocacy is about speaking up for oneself (self-advocacy) and so is concerned with confronting 'that dependent status itself and empowering children to take action themselves' (p. 37). This links to the liberationist perspective on children's rights.

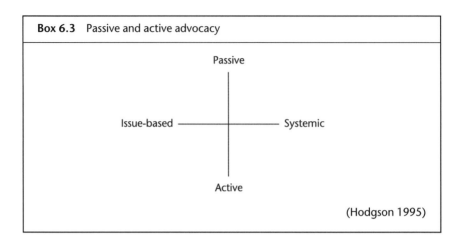

**Box 6.3**  Passive and active advocacy

Passive

Issue-based ——————————— Systemic

Active

(Hodgson 1995)

Hodgson suggests that a continuum is needed for two reasons: first, in practice, both approaches are likely to be used and, second, because of the varying views about what 'true advocacy' is, and 'in particular how far the notion of advocacy presupposes a recognition of rights' (Hodgson 1995: 123). It could be argued that the advocacy role of health and welfare professionals discussed in Chapter 1 is more likely to be at the passive end of the continuum. Hodgson also makes the distinction between issue-based and systemic (which he calls collective) advocacy and notes that, as described in the model above, they are invariably linked.

We can see in Tania and Susie's story in Box 6.4, opposite that, due to their age, some of the advocacy is at the passive end of the continuum where the advocate is liaising with the social worker. However, there is also an element of active advocacy here where the advocate is working directly with Tania and Susie to prepare for their meeting. Hodgson's model therefore acknowledges that both issue-based and systemic advocacy may be at different points of the active–passive continuum, depending on the situation and context of the advocacy support needed.

### Service model

> We're renegotiating it (the Service Level Agreement) and the local authority will put in specific bits of work they want us to do, which will divert time away from the advocacy service because of limited resources. But the local authority has blocked an advocacy referral because they said it would be in contempt of court, and we could not speak to them . . . There are serious questions concerning our independence.
>
> (Lisa, advocacy service manager, in Oliver 2008: 33)

---

**Box 6.4**  Tania and Susie's story

---

Tania and Susie, twins aged 7 years, were looked after by the local authority because of concerns about their neglect at home. They had been in their current placement for nearly a month. The foster carer then asked the advocacy service to visit because the girls were very distressed. They didn't understand why they were in care; they were worried about their cat and other personal possessions and about where their Mother was living and when they could see her. They wanted to know when they could return to their old school. The advocate liaised with the social worker and tried to arrange a visit for the girls to see their Mother. She struggled to get the social worker to understand the urgency of reassuring Tania and Susie. The advocate helped the two girls to prepare what they wanted to say at their fist review and agreed to attend to support them in the meeting.

Case study adapted from Memorandum submitted by the
Children's Advocacy Consortium to the House of Commons Children,
Schools and Families Committee (2008: Ev31)

---

As we discussed in Chapter 4, many advocacy providers are either wholly or partly funded by local authorities, which has an impact on how advocacy is provided. Access to advocacy support within formal mechanisms such as reviews, complaints procedures and child protection conferences to support young people are deemed to be credible. These are systems constituted by service providers as decision-making forums where children and young people are encouraged to participate. However, where advocates position themselves alongside a child or young person to confront the power of organizations, the advocacy role is more likely to be criticized and viewed with suspicion (Dalrymple 2003).

Furthermore, the imperative to achieve results as efficiently as possible (within the 'best value'[4] culture) has, it has been argued, had an impact on both the regulation of advocacy and on its principles and practice (Henderson and Pochin 2001). Finding themselves part of the 'contract culture' has led advocacy services to follow a service model of advocacy (Box 6.5).

Henderson and Pochin (2001) suggest that spot purchasing[5] of advocacy demonstrates how funders have influenced the development of advocacy. The implications of this, they suggest, are that local authorities gatekeep advocacy and remove most of its independence as a result. Furthermore, if there is no core funding for advocacy providers who concentrate solely on advocacy, then inevitably they will have to gain income through providing additional services, which in turn is likely to dilute the provision of good advocacy. Finally, such a linear approach only relates to issue-based advocacy and as such

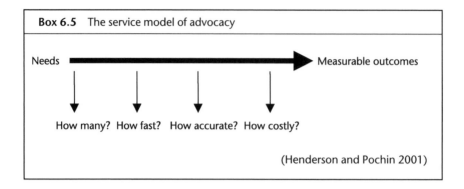

**Box 6.5**   The service model of advocacy

Needs ➤ Measurable outcomes

How many?  How fast?  How accurate?  How costly?

(Henderson and Pochin 2001)

does not really recognize other areas of the work of advocacy services such as systemic advocacy.

## A model for advocacy schemes

Having identified the problems with the service model, Henderson and Pochin (2001) propose a model for advocacy schemes (projects) that takes into account the following:

- values are placed at the heart of the process;
- there is a more inclusive context for advocacy – rather than focus on issues of ownership and principles (as happens in debates about the different forms of advocacy) or on practice and outcomes (as in the service model); and
- funding and funders are deliberately excluded from the model.

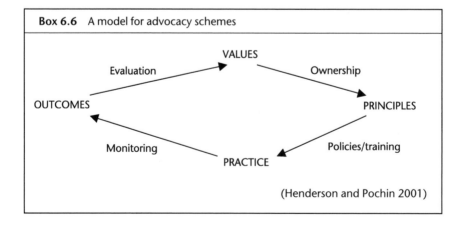

**Box 6.6**   A model for advocacy schemes

VALUES

Evaluation        Ownership

OUTCOMES                    PRINCIPLES

Monitoring        Policies/training

PRACTICE

(Henderson and Pochin 2001)

Henderson and Pochin's detailed description of this model inevitably includes a discussion about the impact of funding, but essentially what they state they are trying to do here is to map the foundations of an advocacy culture and suggest ways in which advocacy can remain independent while assuring a quality service. Let us look briefly at each element of the model using the National Standards for the Provision of Children's Advocacy Services (Standards) to illustrate the points. The starting point is obviously *values*, since advocacy 'begins with a vision, not a series of prescribed tasks' (Henderson and Pochin 2001: 83). While the vision is unlikely to be the same across all advocacy projects, all are underpinned by a commitment to principles of social justice and children's rights. Standard 2 places rights 'at the heart of successful advocacy' (Department of Health 2002: 5), stating that 'Advocacy champions the rights and needs of children and young people'. The core principles guiding the Standards are informed by children and young people:

- Advocates should work for children and young people and no-one else.
- Advocates should value and respect children and young people as individuals and challenge all types of unlawful discrimination.
- Advocates should work to make sure that children and young people in care can understand what is happening to them, can make their views known and, where possible, exercise choice when decisions are being made about them.
- Advocates should help children and young people to raise issues and concerns about things they are unhappy about. This includes making informal and formal complaints under Section 26 of the Children Act 1989.
  (Department of Health 2002; Welsh Assembly Government 2003)

Issues of *ownership* and control in advocacy services for children are complex. Most advocacy services are instigated and managed by adults, who inevitably have their own (adult) agendas, however child focused the aims of the service are. Debates about ownership link back to values, and the ownership of core values 'begin to turn aspirations into realities' (Henderson and Pochin 2001: 84). Standard 8 states that 'Advocacy listens to the views and ideas of children and young people in order to improve the service provided'. This means that an advocacy service that recognizes the benefits of involving children and young people in its management or steering committee is more likely to have shared ownership and value the experiences of children and young people in developing the services. Clearly, how far their participation is meaningful both to the young people involved and to the service will have an impact on the degree of ownership felt.

The Standards can also be seen as a set of guiding *principles* but each project will also have a primary aim, such as to provide advocates for young people in child protection conferences (short-term issue based) or to link a young person with a citizen advocate (long-term relationship).

*Policies* guide the practice of any project. Key standards include:

- Standard 7: 'The Advocacy Service operates to a high level of confidentiality and ensures that children, young people and other agencies are aware of its confidentiality policies'.
- Standard 3: 'All Advocacy Services have clear policies to promote equalities issues and monitor services to ensure that no young person is discriminated against due to age, gender, race, culture, religion, language, disability or sexual orientation'.
- Standard 9: 'The Advocacy Service has an effective and easy to use complaints procedure'.

Standard 10 incorporates the need for projects to have both written policies in nine key areas and that all personnel working in the advocacy organization are trained to a high standard. It specifies areas that need to be covered in any advocacy training.

The *practice and credibility* of a project will be defined by the stages outlined so far – so the management, principles and policies are likely to be a resource when practice is challenged. The findings of national advocacy studies (Oliver et al. 2005; Pithouse et al. 2005) indicate the wide diversity of practice between different advocacy projects. All forms of practice need to be credible however – this involves credibility with service users, commissioners of services and other professionals, and in the systemic advocacy role with policy makers and legislators. The credibility of the project and will have an impact on advocacy practice. Defining and measuring advocacy *outcomes* is controversial and often dictated through service level agreements. *Monitoring and evaluating* advocacy projects is therefore crucial both to ensure the financial sustainability of projects and to inform the development of theory and practice. While all the standards can be used to inform monitoring and evaluation of projects, Standard 10 states that advocacy is 'well managed and gives value for money'.

## The advocacy bridge

Drawing on the concept of building a bridge of participation (Taylor and Upward 1995; John 1996) and the notion of communicative action spaces (Percy-Smith 2006) outlined in Chapter 3, we have developed a model of advocacy that brings together elements of both the theory and practice of advocacy and recognizes the dynamic and ever-changing nature of this process. The model essentially is that of a bridge that crosses the divide between adults and children and young people to bring the two groups together. Initially, the bridge requires a firm foundation. The promotion of advocacy takes place within a children's rights agenda that informs the values and beliefs underpinning advocacy and therefore provides the foundation for the model. Such a foundation is recognized in the National Standards for the Provision of Children's Advocacy Services (Department of Health 2002; Welsh Assembly Government 2003), which clearly state the centrality of Article 12 of the UNCR and the Human Rights Act 1998. In practice, advocates are also clear about this remit:

> Our advocacy work is underpinned by the UN Convention of the Rights of the Child – Article 12 – and that children have rights to express their views and to have their views taken seriously.
>
> (Peter, advocate, in Oliver 2008: 128)

> I come from a children's rights model and use legal documentation to provide a mandate to get people to provide services. I have used Article 12 of the UN Convention and Section 17 of the Children Act to argue that a disabled child is a child in need and is therefore entitled to a service that the social worker is saying they shouldn't have.
>
> (Advocate, in Knight and Oliver 2007: 422)

The bridge has four supporting structures:

- Participation
- Legislation
- Developing knowledge about the theory of advocacy
- Developing knowledge about the practice of advocacy.

The foundation of children's rights and the component parts of the four pillars form a culture of advocacy that enables children and young people to connect with adults across the bridge. To promote a culture of advocacy means that all adults involved in working with children and young people need to understand and be committed to the knowledge, ideas, values and beliefs that constitute the basis of advocacy. Within advocacy services, therefore, a culture of advocacy must be developed that 'accepts the role that advocacy on behalf of clients can play. Otherwise, workers can be unreasonably resistant to suggestions or demands made by clients through advocacy' (Payne 1995: 193). The flow across the bridge needs to be constant and developed in both directions, through ongoing dialogue and exchange between adults and children and young people and within the community of advocates. The bridge therefore needs to be well maintained as well as being built on firm foundations. The maintenance occurs through issue-based advocacy and systemic advocacy, with all parties negotiating together in a process where the young people are not passive but active constructors and maintainers of the bridge. This is assisted by research and evaluation of advocacy services, which contributes to maintaining the supporting structures through critically reflecting on and interrogating the theory and practice of advocacy, promoting participation and influencing policy and legislation.

The strength of the bridge depends on both central and local government agendas and priorities, which will depend on which political party is in power and on government responses to particular issues (e.g. the death of a young person or the abuse of children and young people living away from home). For example, Pithouse et al. (2005) found that short-term contracts for advocacy projects offered little room for manoeuvre, especially for small projects (the majority). Their research found that as social welfare services changed – more children being looked after for shorter periods, more reliance on foster care, more children living out of their local authority area – the demands on advocacy and on their funds increased. This meant that:

> advocacy providers tended to re-target their narrow resource to where risk and visibility combined to shape an agenda around looked after children and child protection, which 'made sense' to local authorities but as a consequence other priorities identified in service level agreements such as children with a disability and other children in need, tended to get displaced.
>
> (Pithouse and Crowley 2008: 141)

The strength of the bridge also depends on the time, resources and personnel available to advocacy services; the flexibility of the agendas of both children and young people and adults; and how far advocates are able to reach out to young people on one side and adult decision-making processes on the other. Integral to this model is the notion of movement and space. The flow across the bridge facilitates the dialogue necessary to create a climate of mutual respect, which will in turn contribute to creating a culture of advocacy. The flow also brings together communities and therefore creates the space for children and young people to work together with adults in a negotiated and cooperative way.

## Summary

Advocacy practice is complex, working within different contexts of practice and changing as knowledge and understanding of advocacy develops.

Consideration of theoretical models helps us to understand the process of advocacy and explain the relationships between the different components within the process. The models examined in this chapter address different elements of advocacy practice as a way of making sense of varying perspectives on children's rights and the legislative and policy mandates that impact on how advocacy services operate. In the advocacy bridge, we have brought together elements of models of participation and advocacy to make sense of contemporary advocacy practice. This model connects the theory and practice of advocacy with ongoing debates to stimulate the dialogue needed to promote a culture of advocacy.

## Notes

1   This was completed by Designs for Change in Chicago and focused on field studies of eight groups working on 52 state and local advocacy activities directed at school reform to benefit vulnerable children.
2   UCAN was an advocacy service for children and young people based in Wales.
3   In 2002, the Welsh Assembly Government set up a Task and Finish Group made up of commissioners and providers to advise on the development of advocacy in Wales.
4   'Best value' means that local authorities are expected to 'secure continuous improvement in the way in which they exercise their functions, having regard to a combination of economy, efficiency and effectiveness' (Local Government Act 1999, p. 3).
5   Where advocacy does not receive core funding, local authority managers may individually 'spot' purchase advocacy from a service provider through a one-off payment.

# 7 Advocacy as a tool for anti-oppressive practice

> Nothing was really done because I was young and people didn't believe me and my sister and brother.
>
> (Young person in consultation for Total Respect, CROA 2000)

We have discussed advocacy in the previous chapters alongside discourses of childhood, children's rights, power, participation, voice and resistance. This positions advocates (whether independent advocates or other professionals taking an advocacy role as part of their practice) as critical practitioners committed to social justice and promoting social change. In Chapter 4, advocacy was described as a controversial and politically daring practice, which indicates its radical potential and usefulness as a tool for promoting change in attitudes towards children and young people and systemic change in the provision of children's services. As such, we argue that advocacy can be viewed as a tool for anti-oppressive practice.

It has been suggested that 'anti-oppressive practice is about making sure that people are never silenced' (Dalrymple and Burke 1995: 162). This commitment to promote the voice and political agency of service users fits well with the values of advocacy that we will discuss later in this chapter. Anti-oppressive practice in relation to children and young people can be described as a radical approach that is informed by humanistic and social justice values and takes account of their experiences and views. It is based on an understanding of how the concepts of power, oppression and inequality determine personal and structural relations. Anti-oppressive practice is based on the belief that services for children and young people should make a difference (Dalrymple and Burke 2000). The following pointers for anti-oppressive practice, which are adapted from work by Clifford and others (Clifford 1995; Burke and Harrison 1998; Clifford and Burke 2001), draw on black feminist and other non-dominant perspectives. These principles can help to develop thinking about anti-oppressive practice and advocacy and underpin the work of advocates through:

- analysis of social difference with attention to the varying power relations between children/young people and adults and other differences that interact in the lives of all those involved in advocacy work with children and young people;
- evaluation of the differing kinds of power dimensions that arise in situations where children and young people require advocacy support;
- evaluation of the different effects and levels of interacting systems in the circumstances in which children and young people seek advocacy support.
- consideration of how personal and organizational histories lead to and mould the understanding and behaviour of those involved in the receipt and provision of advocacy;
- analysis of the mutual interaction between advocates and the children and young people involved (reflexivity).

To contextualize advocacy in relation to anti-oppressive practice, we therefore begin by briefly looking at the values of advocacy. We go on to think about principles of empowerment before moving on to discuss the notion of advocates as critical practitioners. Finally, we look at the structures within which advocacy predominantly operates and think about the issues for advocates working with commissioners of advocacy services.

## Advocacy values

> We live in a world dominated by adult values. Children's rights are a political as well as a moral issue and they can conflict with adult authority that oppresses children and denies opportunities that all children should enjoy in safety.
>
> (Utting 1997: 3)

For advocates and practitioners working with the ambiguities and complexities inherent in the lives of children and young people who seek advocacy support, it is necessary to engage in critical debate about personal, professional and organizational values. This enables us to consider the nature and scope of advocacy practice as well as thinking about the intersection of these values. Agreeing a set of values that relate to advocates working with vulnerable children and young people is not without its difficulties. Values have been described as 'a set of beliefs, ideas and assumptions that both individuals and groups hold about themselves and the society they live in. Values are a part of the culture and societal norms that guide people's daily lives' (Eby 2000: 18), and they are used to refer 'to one or all of religious, moral, political or ideological principles, beliefs or attitudes' (Banks 2001: 6).

Drawing on values outlined by Atkinson (1999) and the core principles from the National Standards for the Provision of Advocacy Service set out in Box 7.1 (Department of Health 2002; Welsh Assembly Government 2003), we suggest that advocacy practice encapsulates the following value statements:

- a commitment to social justice;
- respect for children and young people;
- valuing uniqueness and diversity;
- empowering children and young people to come to voice;
- challenging the discrimination and oppression of children and young people.

Advocates can, however, find that they have to consider competing and sometimes contradictory values. For example, an independent advocate's own values may well conflict with the values of the advocacy service. Similarly, professionals taking on an advocacy role may find there is a tension between their own values and the values of the organization in which they are working. Children and young people also have their value positions.

---

**Box 7.1**  Core principles set out in the National Advocacy Standards for the Provision of Advocacy Services

- Advocates should work for children and young people and no one else;
- Advocates should value and respect children and young people as individuals and challenge all types of unlawful discrimination;
- Advocates should work to make sure that children and young people in care can understand what is happening to them, can make their views known and, where possible, exercise choice when decisions about them are being made;
- Advocates should help children and young people to raise issues and concerns about things they are unhappy about. This includes making informal and formal complaints under Section 26 of the Children Act 1989.

---

Box 7.2 illustrates some dilemmas that could arise in advocacy practice. By critically reflecting on the various value positions, advocates working with children and young people can examine how different discourses impact on their decision making. For example, the dominance of the 'best interests' paradigm could be influencing both Richard and Ciara in different ways. Apart from their perception of whether or not they are condoning absence from school, Richard's values could be influenced by his personal experiences of

---

**Box 7.2**   Exercise: Advocacy values

---

*Richard and Ciara are two advocates working in the same advocacy service. Both are working with young people who do not always attend school. Richard has been working with Martha (age 12) since she was excluded from school. Part of the difficulties Martha had in school related to bullying. Richard has been working with Martha to enable her to have her views, wishes and feelings heard by the school. They have devised a plan to ensure that she has a smooth transition back into school. However, Martha finds attending school on a regular basis difficult. She recently phoned Richard during the school day asking him to visit. He agreed to see her but insisted that this would be at the end of the school day as she really should be in school. This is his practice with all the young people he works with who should be attending school – even if they are at home he will not visit until after school hours. Ciara, on the other hand, has no problem with meeting with young people when they should be at school. Although she respects Richard's value position, she also finds that this makes her working day easier and also her personal value position does not place such emphasis on rigid school attendance for young people who may have been bullied or are experiencing other difficulties. She also argues that she is trying to respect the decision of the young person in choosing not to attend school.*

Think about how Richard and Ciara's personal values and beliefs contribute to the way that they work as advocates.

What aspects of their life experiences may have had an impact on their different approaches to working with Martha?

To help you with this, you may like to think about your own experiences in relation to school:

- What were your parents'/carers' attitudes to the value of education and attending school? Can you identify what may have influenced their attitudes?
- Are there gender differences in how education is perceived and valued?
- Where did you go to school – private or public, local or residential? Was it a single-sex school, a faith-based school? Or were you educated at home?
- What are your own attitudes to the value of education and attending school?
- Can you identify any experiences which enable you to critically reflect on the values that you hold about education and attending school?

education and a belief that it is in Martha's best interests to attend while Ciara could actually believe that it is in her best interests not to attend.

In our discussions about children's rights in Chapter 2, we examined protectionist and liberationist perspectives. If we think about values in relation to these perspectives, we can see that there is a tension between their different orientations relating to children's and young people's rights. Similarly, the UNCRC, which underpins advocacy practice, can be seen both as a key instrument for improving the lives of children and young people and a critical landmark in the development of children's rights, but it is also based on protectionist principles. Article 3 is an interesting one to reflect on here – this provides that the best interests of the child shall be the primary consideration in all decisions taken concerning the child. Kilkelly and Lundy (2006) point out that since this principle is not clearly defined in the UNCRC, its application in practice varies according to individual or organizational values in areas such as child care, education and youth justice. The UNCRC and legislation such as the Children Act 1989, the Children Act 2004, the Children (Scotland) Act 1995 and the Children (Northern Ireland) Order 1995 are tools that advocates can use to promote anti-oppressive practice. However, in promoting the rights of children and young people we also need to be aware of competing discourses of childhood as outlined in Chapter 2. Nevertheless, the legislation does enshrine the rights of children and young people to be actively involved in decision making.

Practice that is underpinned by the five value statements set out above can be strengthened by integrating principles of anti-oppressive practice and ensure that the passion and determination of advocates is maintained to ensure the rights of children and young people are respected and their voices listened to, heard and responded to. Using Marcus's story set out in Box 7.3, we will briefly analyse his situation in the light of the principles set out at the start of the chapter by way of illustration.

In this scenario it would be easy to see Marcus merely as a young black person in prison who is homeless. However, an advocate would need to consider Marcus's situation as a young person who has experienced the care system, has already experienced a period of homelessness and has suffered a number of losses – for example, he has been separated from his mother, he has lost his home and his liberty. He has also been rejected by his aunt. These will feed into the power dimensions that are being played out. His mother, his aunt, the Judiciary, the Prison Service, the Housing Department, Social Services, Connexions and the Youth Offending Team (YOT) all shape and determine individual relationships, organizational and community relationships at various levels. The advocate needs to take into account their own powers, what power Marcus has and the power of the interacting systems. We can see that the YOT worker recognized the limitations of his power and used this understanding to suggest to Marcus that the support of an advocate would

---

**Box 7.3**   Case study: Marcus

Marcus is a 16-year-old black young person who was looked after by local author-ity foster carers between the ages of 12 and 14. His mother, Philomena, whose parents moved to England from Ghana when she was 4 years old, has bi-polar disorder and is a single parent. When Marcus was 14 he returned to live with Philomena, and things initially went well. However, unknown to Marcus, Philomena's debts had been escalating, she found it increasingly difficult to cope and this affected her mental health. Shortly after Marcus's fifteenth birthday they were evicted from the family home and Philomena moved to live with her sister. However, because Marcus had an ASBO (Anti-Social Behaviour Order)[1], the family did not feel that they wanted to offer Marcus accommodation as well. This left him homeless and he tried to manage on his own for a while, sleeping at friends' houses and sleeping rough. Marcus did not want to approach Social Services for help as he did not want to go back into care. During this time he became involved in a serious fight resulting in a charge of actual bodily harm, for which he received a twelve-month Detention and Training Order which he served at a young offender institution.

Prior to his release, Marcus expressed concerns about having nowhere to live. He spoke to a worker from the Youth Offending Team (YOT)[2] about what he needed to do to get a flat. The YOT worker discussed the need to complete a housing application but was also aware that Marcus would need to report as homeless on release and told Marcus that he might need to continue to rely on his friends for a while. However, the worker was also concerned about Marcus's general well-being and the danger that he might get into trouble again without support and somewhere to live. On contacting Social Services, the YOT worker was told that the case was closed and as Marcus was now 16 he was classed as an adult. The YOT worker then talked to Marcus about the advocacy service available and Marcus agreed to talk to an advocate who regularly visited the young offender institution.

The advocate made a new referral to Social Services. However, he was informed that they could not offer anything more than the services provided through the Youth Offending Team and Connexions. The advocate then wrote to the local authority legal department reminding them that they had a duty to undertake a 'child-in-need assessment' with a view to providing accommodation for Marcus under Section 20 of the Children Act 1989. The outcome was that Social Services did undertake an assessment prior to Marcus's release and agreed to provide accommodation for him. The advocate was then able to explore with Marcus other support that he might need.

be helpful. The YOT worker would be aware of the independence of the advocate in contrast to his own position within the organizational structures. The advocate experienced powerlessness in the initial contact with Social Services, but was also able to use knowledge of the system to resist their response. It is also interesting to reflect on the power of 'status' here – Marcus has been variously labelled as a 'looked after child', a 'child in need' and a 'young offender'. These labels have the potential to mask Marcus's strengths and resilience:

- he had lived with a parent who experienced mental health problems;
- he had experienced being homeless;
- at the age of 15 he made a conscious choice to try and take control of his own life without the help of Social Services;
- while in prison, however, he recognized the need to seek help to find somewhere to live.

Here, the advocate's role is issue-based and task-centred. However, Marcus's experience of being listened to and valued and the eventual positive outcome may lead him to position the advocate and the YOT worker as loyal friends, particularly in view of his recent negative experiences of other adults (Dalrymple 2004a). The advocate therefore needs to be reflective and reflexive while working with Marcus.

Reflexivity is described as 'the continual consideration of how values, social difference and power affect the interactions between individuals' (Burke and Harrison 1998: 229), which would enable the advocate to understand and locate the nature of her or his relationship with Marcus. Marcus is a young black male who is likely to be disaffected by society as a result of his experiences. A female advocate would need to consider Marcus's attitude to women, particularly as he has been let down by both his mother and his aunt. Philomena was the head of the household and so Marcus may have a particular view of black women and of women in authority. A female advocate would therefore be mindful of her own power in this situation and how Marcus might react to this, even if she is engaging respectfully with him and working with Marcus to improve his situation. This is likely to impact on the relationship between Marcus and the advocate. We do not know what his experiences were of parenting in foster care – however, understanding his experiences of foster care and thinking about the ethnicity of his carers is clearly important. A male advocate would also be mindful of these issues but there is an additional dimension in the power relations between two men. If Marcus has been part of a violent gang culture, he may have specific views about men and masculinity and his own identity as a young black man. His determination to manage to live independently not only reflects the situation in which he found himself, but also a level of pride and his self-identity as a young black adult who could and should be able to survive on his own. A key issue here for an advocate, therefore, is to think about how their own gender and ethnicity will affect the interaction between the two. Furthermore, an advocate is likely to have his or her own feelings and values about violent crime, which will impact on how they engage with a young black man involved in a violent offence. It is important to be aware of and recognize any fear that we might feel when we are working with children and young people in difficult situations. There is a tension here for advocates who are committed both to the five values identified earlier and to challenging the oppression and marginalization of children and young people, but who also experience feelings that appear to 'judge and oppress' young people like Marcus. This may mean that they fail to understand the pain he has experienced and is likely still to be feeling, which in turn is likely to have an impact on how they hear his voice (Ferguson 2005; Dalrymple and Burke 2006).

## Advocacy and empowerment

In our examination of definitions of advocacy in Chapter 4, we discussed how children and young people seeking advocacy support may feel disempowered by the systems and processes they encounter. For example, the isolation experienced by frequent moves can result in a sense of powerlessness and an inability to influence decision making. A move from long-term established placements can be particularly emotionally distressing and disruptive for young people. This may be compounded if the move is from a long-term foster placement, which the young person regards as home, to the alien environment of a residential children's home. Suraya's story in Box 7.4 reflects feelings of loss, and having no power or control over events in her life. While we argue that empowerment is only one element of advocacy practice and is not sufficient on its own, by enabling children and young people like Suraya to influence decision-making empowerment practice can be seen as a strategy for promoting equality through challenging injustice and oppression. Exploring the process of empowerment is therefore helpful in understanding advocacy as a tool for anti-oppressive practice.

A number of commentators discuss empowerment practice taking place at different levels. Let us look briefly at how this operates in relation to advocacy practice. Essentially, empowerment practice can occur at three levels. The first level relates to the individual experiences of children and young people. Young people's thoughts and feelings are likely to affect how they experience inequality and oppression. At this level the role of an advocate is to enable children and young people to share relevant views and opinions about their situation. Rees (1991) discusses how the process of telling the story is significant in itself, as is the way that service users are heard – he calls this the 'promise of biography'. In that process, young people become more confident

---

**Box 7.4**   Case study: Suraya

Suraya entered the care system as a baby and was placed with foster carers. Suraya remained with the same foster carers, in the same house, attending local schools until she was fourteen years old. She remembers this as a really happy time. She had plans to go to college when she left school. However, Suraya remembers that sadly there were problems, which resulted in the placement ending. Over the following two years Suraya experienced a great deal of change and disruption in her life. She was moved to a number of residential children's homes, an environment she was not comfortable with. Suraya vividly remembers being moved at short notice, having her belongings moved from place to place in a black bin bag, and feeling a mixture of anger and despair. She disliked the lack of privacy, changes in staff and feeling that she had no-one just for her. When she was sixteen she recalls being initially 'put into' a flat. Suraya felt unsupported and ill-prepared for the experience. Unable to cope she was evicted and moved into supported lodgings, an arrangement which quickly broke down. Suraya was then placed into 'independent living' in a hostel for homeless young people. She had items of her belongings stolen, experienced financial hardship but she would still like to go to college.

(Boylan 2005: 112)

---

as they feel valued and taken seriously, which is of itself experienced as empowering. Since many children and young people who work with an advocate have previously felt unable to engage in meaningful dialogue with an adult, the need for advocates to create a 'communicative action space' as outlined by Percy-Smith (2006) is helpful here.

The second level is about self-awareness. As children and young people begin to gain knowledge about themselves and reflect on their situation, they can work with an advocate or talk with other children and young people in similar circumstances (as in peer advocacy) and find ways of thinking about moving from feeling powerless to feeling more able to change the situation. To move beyond the personal level we need to think about the cultural context of children's and young people's lives. As the connections are made between their own biographies and those of others, children and young people will gain insight and self-knowledge about their situation. Finally, the third level relates to systemic advocacy in which children and young people with advocacy support work towards changing wider social and political structures. At this level, the goal is invariably about changing legislation, policy and practice, but it may also be about small changes that affect the life of an individual child or young person.

---

**Box 7.5**   Experiences of child protection conferences

---

*When you turn up the Chair is really welcoming but when the meeting has started it just goes into job mode. Also it is a bit kind of jargon or talk in initials. Neither the young person or I know what the initials mean – I wonder if they are important . . .*

*. . . they listen and . . . it made no difference*

*I swear some of them didn't listen. They butted in.*

*I don't think they did really take notice. [The advocate] pointed out things wrong in the report.*

(Comments taken from fieldwork notes for evaluation of Child
Protection Conferences in Wiltshire, Dalrymple 2005)

---

The comments in Box 7.5 identify the impact of attending child protection conferences on both advocates and children and young people. In this instance, we can see that for the 'promise of biography' to be realized, the whole child protection process needs to be a 'communicative space' characterized by respect, justice and equality. The following quotation from a local authority representative encapsulates the challenge and recognizes the need to combine issue-based and systemic advocacy as part of the process of empowerment:

> Promoting justice for children and young people in the child protec-
> tion system has also been a challenge for advocacy. Respect for chil-
> dren and young people's rights has strengthened however with
> 'advocacy at both the case and policy level influencing the direction
> of child protection services.

(Wyllie 2000: 6)

## Advocacy, anti-oppressive practice and the critical practitioner

Thinking about advocacy and critical practice provides the opportunity to conceive of practice as less about what power it is that the advocate has, and more about how they use the opportunities available to them within varying contexts of practice. 'Critical practice' means being open-minded and reflec-tive, 'taking account of different perspectives, experiences and assumptions' (Glaister 2008: 9). Principles of critical practice sit well with advocacy, particularly significant being the fact that critical practitioners must empower and make a difference to the lives of service users (Adams et al. 2000). In their exposition of critical practice, Adams et al. (2002) take Brechin's work further in a way that is very relevant to systemic advocacy. They suggest that 'making a difference' goes beyond the individual to thinking about empowering oppressed groups in society – the critical practitioner sees the link between issue-based and systemic advocacy as important.

Advocates working with children and young people from a critical perspective need to recognize that the concept of critical practice is underpinned by the following assumptions:

- Social and organizational structures such as families, schools or children's health and welfare services are not fixed and immutable.
- Children and young people's voices give meaning to their circumstances and their perspectives have consequences.
- Interpersonal relationships and structures have an impact on adult-child/young people power relations which can be exposed and held to account.
- Different approaches and outcomes can be explored and sometimes achieved.

(Glaister 2008)

In Chapter 4, we saw that change is central to advocacy practice. It is also central to practice that is anti-oppressive. This is encapsulated in the following definition of advocacy:

> Advocacy is a process for change, a process for learning. It stimulates respect for children's and young people's rights and promotes participation in the planning and challenging of the systems that impact on their lives. Acting on children's and young people's experiences and views, the advocacy extends beyond individual casework.
> (UCAN Annual Report 2004–2005)

Our examination of advocacy has been underpinned by thinking about adult/child power relations and the oppression of children and young people by adults and by systems. Consideration of the potential for organizational structures, policies and practice to be oppressive is a starting point and, within that, acknowledging that as adults we all have a responsibility to rethink the relationship between organizations and young people to challenge their oppression. This is difficult, as funding arrangements for advocacy services mean that particular groups of children and young people are targeted and therefore access to advocacy is determined by the organizational structures that determine how advocacy services are provided. Furthermore, research has raised concerns about the reach of advocacy – for example, despite a service being available to looked after children and young people, those from ethnic minority backgrounds, disabled children and younger children may be denied a service because the advocacy service does not have sufficient resources, skills or knowledge to meet their needs (Oliver 2008). Similarly, research relating to young people in Wales making complaints about health services noted that ad hoc arrangements for unsupported children or young people with disabilities were unlikely to ensure effective access to the system either to make a complaint or be supported by an advocate in the process, and support for travellers, refugees and asylum seekers was limited (Payne and Pithouse 2006). More generally, research in Wales identified significant difficulties in providing advocacy support for disabled children, children out of a local authority area, those in short-term respite care and children living with foster carers (Pithouse and Parry 2005). This may well be because, as Oliver's research demonstrates, advocates are predominantly white and female and only a minority 'describe themselves as having a disability' (Oliver 2008: 39). This is of concern in view of the fact that, as one advocate in Oliver's research reported, 80 per cent of the users of the advocacy service in a six-month period were black and ethnic minority children and young people. Despite attempts therefore through Standard 3 of the National Standards for the Provision of Children's Advocacy Services[3] to ensure that advocacy services are socially inclusive, children and young people are going to continue to be oppressed by the very services that are also trying to challenge their oppression.

The research and evaluation of advocacy therefore has a key part to play in understanding the situation of advocacy at a given time and the factors influencing the development of advocacy (Oliver and Dalrymple 2008). This can contribute both to understanding the potential for advocacy services to become part of oppressive systems and, importantly, to the theorizing of advocacy. Recent theorizing about advocacy practice has developed what might be described as a more critical approach. Such an approach is described as:

> primarily concerned with practising in ways which further a society without domination, exploitation and oppression. It will focus on how structures dominate, but also on how people construct and are constructed by changing social structures and relations, recognising that there may be multiple and diverse constructions of ostensibly similar situations. Such an understanding of social relations and structures can be used to disrupt dominant understandings and structure, and as a basis for changing these so that they are more inclusive of different interest groups.
>
> (Fook 2002: 18)

We have discussed how discourses of childhood, rights and power can operate to marginalize and oppress children and young people. So, for example, the language used by some adults can exclude children and young people and, in more subtle ways, exclude their advocates (Dalrymple 2003). If advocacy is to challenge the oppression and resist the marginalization of children and young people, then advocates as critical practitioners need to appreciate the power of dominant discourses. Understanding and recognizing the prominence of the 'best interests' paradigm is a useful example here.

From this analysis we can see that adult advocates need to understand the subtleties of oppressive structures and the potential that they could also become part of those oppressive structures. While writers have expressed concern about the potential for advocacy to be oppressive (Solomon 1976; Wilson and Beresford 2000; Fook 2002), the professional expertise of advocates who are able to manage the complexity of varying contexts of practice provides the opportunity for advocacy to be a tool for anti-oppressive practice – to challenge constructions of children and childhood. For example, family group conferences[4] have the potential to oppress young people as much any other decision-making forum. The role of an advocate in a family group conference is to work with the young person to ensure that both familial and professional power is confronted (Dalrymple 2007). This then locates advocates as critical practitioners who understand 'how the concepts of power, oppression and inequality determine personal and structural relations' (Dalrymple and Burke 1995: 56).

## Anti-oppressive practice and working with commissioners of services

The attitudes of service providers are often articulated through discourses that serve to create distance between young people and advocates, and between providers and young people with their advocates. Equally subtle is the control of advocacy through gatekeeping access to its services and constructing advocacy from adult-centred perspectives rather than child-centred perspectives. This confirms the need for *adult* advocates to support children and young people within adult-controlled systems, but reminds us of the dangers for advocates who may also be disempowered by the systems. Their exclusion by other professionals could lead them to look for ways of working within the systems which would then distance them from the young people requiring advocacy support. This leads us to consider ways of articulating the need for a culture of advocacy to challenge the construction of advocacy by commissioners of advocacy services. Payne acknowledges early thinking in this respect when he writes:

> Within service-providing organisations, a 'culture of advocacy' (Dalrymple 1993) must be built up which accepts the role that

advocacy on behalf of clients can play. Otherwise, workers can be unreasonably resistant to suggestions or demands made by clients through advocacy.

(Payne 1995: 193)

Local authority services such as health, education and social services may all be committed to the provision of advocacy for particular groups of children and young people. It is not unusual, for instance, for a range of independent organizations to be commissioned to provide advocacy for young people in child protection conferences, for looked after children and young people, for young people with autistic spectrum disorder in transition planning, and for children and young people making a complaint, as well as independent mental health advocates. In addition, a children's rights and/or participation worker may also be employed directly by the local authority, as will independent reviewing officers who have a responsibility to ensure that young people are able to participate meaningfully in their looked after reviews. However, this does not necessarily mean that a culture of advocacy exists within the authority. For example, there may often be misunderstandings and a degree of suspicion between child care practitioners committed to an advocacy role as part of their professional expertise and the role of independent advocates, while tensions between advocacy organizations with insecure funding and who are tendering against each other for contracts to provide a service can also contribute to difficult professional relationships and confusion about the advocacy role (Oliver 2008; Parry et al. 2008). Employees of the local authority and commissioned services are therefore likely to be operating independently, possibly unaware of each other's existence, struggling with limited resources to promote an understanding of their role within a small part of the whole organizational structure – and no culture of advocacy. A culture will only begin to develop when a space for dialogue is created both within the community of advocates and with practitioners using advocacy skills within their work. Arguably, an employee such as a children's rights officer is in a key position to enable that dialogue, bringing together all those concerned to enable children and young people to come to voice so that they can dismantle barriers and work together to accept and understand the role of advocacy in the lives of children and young people using services.

The development of a culture of advocacy also has the potential to challenge the proceduralization of advocacy. This has become an emerging concern with the marketization of advocacy and expectations on health, social care and education providers to provide children and young people with access to advocacy services alongside the regulation of advocacy through National Standards (Boylan and Wylie 1999; Parry et al. 2008). The problem here is that in the context of anti-oppressive practice there is a danger that advocacy becomes an extension of the commissioning organization, giving the illusion of being a force for change which could curtail the vision of advocacy in promoting equality and social justice. Guidelines for commissioners of services from the Scottish Executive outlined in Box 7.6 are helpful in raising awareness about this potential. The other aspect of proceduralization is the expectation that children and young people will produce reports for meetings such as reviews or child protection conferences. Our concern is that advocates and young people are then expected to fit into systems, using the same means as professionals to share information, rather than being a force for change.

---

**Box 7.6**   Ten dos and don'ts for commissioning advocacy

### DO

1   Do ensure that independence is built into the project design/service specification.
2   Do involve people who use services, people who are independent of the service system, existing advocacy and rights groups and people with experience of advocacy in deciding what sort of project is needed.
3   Do be clear what you want it to achieve, and that the project you commission will be appropriate to meet that need.
4   Do make sure that it has realistic aims and adequate resources to meet them.
5   Do acknowledge that an advocate's primary loyalty must be to the person or group they are advocating for, not a commissioner or provider of services
6   Do stress that the service provider must make sure that professional staff understand people's need to have access to, and get support from, independent advocates and advocacy groups.
7   Do remember that advocacy will, at times, lead to conflict and put pressure on services to change and adapt to meet individuals' needs.
8   Do remember that people who have been neglected, or ignored, may have difficulty expressing their needs and may be very angry. You may need to work hard to understand what they are saying, and to act appropriately.
9   Do spend time, money and effort helping agencies to develop their proposals.
10   Do remember that it is often better for advocacy groups to do one thing well than to try to meet many different aims and expectations.

### DON'T

1   Don't try to control the advocacy effort. It becomes ineffective when compromised.
2   Don't set advocacy organisations up to fail by putting unreasonable expectations on them.

3   Don't develop plans for advocacy without the active involvement of people who use services or who are independent of the system.
4   Don't forget to provide continued support to advocates and self advocates.
5   Don't think that funding an advocacy organisation is all that needs to be done.
6   Don't forget that participation costs time and money. Volunteers and service users need to have their expenses paid.
7   Don't expect non-professionals to understand the jargon and to be able to complete tenders without help.
8   Don't underestimate how far a little help can go to boost morale and restore trust.
9   Don't expect an advocate or advocacy project to keep silent in the face of injustice.
10   Don't forget how you would feel if your freedom was curtailed and decisions taken for you.

(Scottish Executive 2001)

## Summary

The skills of advocates go beyond an ability to communicate with children and young people, or to manage systems. The critical practitioner recognizes the potential that, with the increasing professionalization of advocacy, it is moving away from the agenda of children and young people and could contribute to the maintenance of unequal systems. While many professionals working with children and young people are committed critical practitioners, it is not always possible for them either to take on the advocacy role or change the systems they are working within. The problem for independent advocates is that they face the danger of becoming aligned with other health and social welfare practitioners, reinforcing the similarities rather than the distinctiveness of advocacy. Despite its radical roots, using advocacy as a tool for anti-oppressive practice is a challenge for advocates. Advocacy expertise therefore involves a complex synthesis of knowledge and skills, underpinned by the values of advocacy if advocates are to work with uncertainty and change and resist their own marginalization within the systems.

## Notes

1   Anti-Social Behaviour Orders (ASBOs), provisions of which are found in Section 1 of the Crime and Disorder Act 1998, are made if, on the balance of

probabilities, the court is satisfied that the person has caused harassment, alarm or distress as defined by the Act.

2   Youth Offending Teams are multidisciplinary teams that include health, social work and educations workers, police and probation. They were set up under the Crime and Disorder Act 1998.

3   Standard 3: 'All Advocacy Services have clear policies to promote equalities issues and monitor services to ensure that no young person is discriminated against due to age, gender, race, culture, religion, language, disability or sexual orientation'.

4   Family group conferences have their origins in New Zealand and bring together the child or young person, family and extended members and friendship networks to address particular issues and attempt to find solutions to them.

# 8    The way forward – optimism and notes of caution

Advocacy in the UK has emerged in the context of children and young people being marginalized and excluded in decision making. The philosophy that underpins advocacy is the belief that children and young people should be recognized and respected as young citizens and as such advocacy is synonymous with the concept of social justice. This has developed as a result of efforts by those advocating for children's and young people's social, civil and political rights. Major policy milestones include the 1924 Geneva Declaration on the Rights of the Child, the 1949 United Nations Declaration of Human Rights, the 1959 United Nations Declaration on the Rights of the Child and the UNCRC 1989.

In an attempt to establish and legitimize advocacy services for children and young people, advocacy campaigners have endeavoured to secure legal mandates for advocacy, on the premise that even with support for the expansion of advocacy, without legislative weight it would 'remain for the most part a fashionable concept' (Sim and Mackay 1997: 11). Legislation does now exist to ensure that in some circumstances children and young people have a legal right to advocacy, and there are ongoing campaigns to extend this. There are, however, problems with legislative mandates in respecting how far a statutory framework will then control the provision and development of advocacy. In the USA, where there is legislative support for a form of child advocacy at state level, there is less financial support than for other public interest groups (Richart and Bing 1989). In Canada, where a number of provinces have legislated for the provision of child and youth advocacy offices, there has been a general erosion of child care services, although the need for a limited budget for advocacy has been identified. Despite being under-resourced, these offices do have the benefit of mandates to ensure that the rights of children are not violated.

In the UK, advocacy for children and young people has become incorporated into children's service plans, quality projects/children first targets and Every Child Matters. It is a huge step forward that a handbook identifying ways of building a culture of participation has been published by the Department for Education and Skills – and furthermore that this recognizes the value of systemic advocacy: 'Developing networks with other professionals, targeting information and advocacy helps disseminate young people's ideas widely and influence change across a range of organisations' (Kirby et al. 2003: 31).

There is a paradox, however, in promoting a legislative mandate for child and youth advocacy. First, the impact of the proceduralization of advocacy on the provision of advocacy services is a real concern (Boylan and Braye 2006). For example, there is a danger that in the provision of advocacy for children and young people involved in child protection proceedings, advocacy services find that they are trying to fit into adult/professional frames of reference rather than promote radical change (Boylan and Wylie 1999; Dalrymple and Horan 2008b). The positive element of a legislative mandate is the recognition that the need for and provision of advocacy for children and young people and advocates is being taken seriously. The difficulty is that while clearly children and young people and their advocates want to be taken seriously, they do not want to be taken over.

Second, advocacy services for children and young people are developing in a framework that is controlled by central government. Clearly, advocacy now has a higher profile within health, welfare and education services. One of the core standards of the National Service Framework for Children, Young People and Maternity Services (DfES 2004) is to 'give children, young people and their parents increased information, power and choice over the support and treatment they receive, and involve them in planning'. These sentiments are echoed by both advocates and professionals working with children and young people. As well as a legal right to advocacy support for looked after children and young people making a complaint, other exciting developments include the introduction of Independent Mental Capacity Advocates (IMCA) through the Mental Health Act 2005 (relevant to young people over the age of 16). This legislation aims to help vulnerable people who lack the capacity to make important decisions about serious medical treatment and changes of accommodation and is a significant development. Young people who have no family or friends to consult about such decisions are able to have the support of an advocate. Two of the five principles underpinning the legislation indicate how the rights of vulnerable people are now being valued:

- Section 1(3) says that a person is not to be treated as unable to make a decision unless all practicable steps to help him or her do so have been taken without success. Even though an IMCA has been instructed, all practicable steps should continue to be taken in an effort to enhance the person's capacity.
- Section 1(4) says that a person is not to be treated as unable to make a decision merely because he or she makes an unwise decision. People

instructing IMCAs will need to confirm that a decision that others might consider to be unwise but made by a person who does in fact have the capacity to make it was not the reason for their instructions. If it were, an IMCA would not be able to act because the person would have capacity – and would be free to make whatever decision they wish.

For children and young people, guidance for teachers working with young people with an autistic disorder indicates the importance of finding ways for children and young people to have a voice:

> Many procedures for assessment, programme planning and review now have sections to be completed by the children themselves. Professionals are developing ways of obtaining the views and opinions of children on all aspects of school life and their future plans. This is a challenge as many individuals with ASDs [autistic spectrum disorders], even those who are able, have difficulties in expressing choices and in decision making. For some children, parents will assess their needs and preferences and speak for them. However, as professionals continue to develop ways for non-verbal and less able children to indicate their choices, an increasing number of children should be involved in making decisions which affect their everyday lives.
>
> (http://www.teachernet.gov.uk/wholeschool/sen/asds/
> asdgoodpractice/Advocacy/)

However, there are tensions between the traditional campaigning role of advocacy and legislation that can constrain and define the development of advocacy and its accessibility to those who need it most. Once a system is incorporated into legislation, it loses its autonomy and becomes bureaucratized and susceptible to change to suit government strategies and the political imperatives. If, as we identified in our consideration of the advocacy role of child care practitioners in Chapter 1, it is becoming increasingly difficult for these professionals to take on the advocacy role or even to promote independent advocacy, then independent advocates who are an integral part of a child welfare system and dependent on local authority funding are likely to find themselves compromised in the same way. For organizations that threaten state power, a legislative mandate increases their vulnerability as they place themselves in a position to be systematically dismantled if necessary (Dalrymple 2004a).

Third, the marketization of advocacy has led to it becoming a commodity that can be bought and sold within a welfare economy (Boylan and Braye 2006). Furthermore, advocacy providers are reliant on contracts for their existence, which can both determine the parameters of the advocacy they provide and create competition between advocacy providers. Pithouse and Crowley (2008) note that in a desire to win contracts, the integrity of advocacy providers could be undermined. Furthermore, short-term contracts may lead to uncertainty for projects in terms of staff and for children and young people. Changing policies and priorities have led to cuts in funding and a struggle to survive. For example, a number of advocacy projects were set up in England using money made available through the Quality Protects programme. Once this ended, some projects were unable to continue. Contracted services rarely provide overheads or development costs, and small voluntary organizations are faced with administrative pressures. Despite this, they are required to maintain any statutory commitments.

Nevertheless, children's and young people's rights have found strengthened expression in legislation in the UK. Advocacy has a role to play in the promotion and monitoring of policies and practices conducive to children's and young people's rights and widening the reach of advocacy to all children and young people. The development of National Standards for the Provision of Advocacy Services (Department of Health 2002; Welsh Assembly Government 2003), introduced to enable the development of high-quality advocacy services, is also an important development in raising the status of advocacy but need to be considered in light of the impact they have on the development of advocacy. In particular, here the threshold of confidentiality is one that is contentious and arguably higher than many advocacy services would choose. Expressing fears about the phraseology of the confidentiality standard, Sir Ronald Waterhouse noted that 'if the advocate/child relationship is to work, however, full weight must be given to the confidentiality principle, as it is in the law' (Waterhouse 2003: 22). While children, young people and advocates want advocacy to be taken seriously and delivered to a high quality, the danger of them becoming controlled and shaped by bureaucratic procedures that fit adult terms of reference is very real. However, again, by way of balance, the core principles underpinning the standards have been informed by children and young people and reflect the importance of ensuring that they are central to the development of advocacy practice.

Overall, it is important that we are not seduced into thinking that advocacy is now 'on the map' and, since it is now incorporated into legislation and policy, all is well. There is evidence from literature that particular groups of young people still do not have access to effective mechanisms for enabling their voice to be heard. For example, the following groups of children and young people may need access to advocacy:

- children and young people at risk of family breakdown, school exclusion, poverty, neglect or abuse;
- all children living away from home, including residential schools, children's homes and foster homes;

- children and young people in secure accommodation or prison;
- children and young people using public services of any kind;
- disabled children and young people, especially those who are living away from home much of the time or who are 'looked after' by local authorities;
- black and ethnic minority children and young people;
- young people leaving care, who are at risk of unemployment, poverty and hardship;
- children and young people who are victims of domestic violence, including those living in refuges and those who are homeless.

There are many forms of advocacy that may be used to support children and young people in different situations. As we saw with 'A' in Chapter 5, situations where young people require support to challenge their oppression by local authorities who will not listen to what they are saying may require support to access legal advocacy and ongoing support to ensure that they know and understand what their rights are. More traditional ways of working are developing alongside newer forms such as non-instructed advocacy and e-advocacy approaches. Advocacy is constantly looking for innovative ways of working to promote the rights of children and young people to come to voice, to be heard and to participate in decision making. Advocacy is an exciting and radical way of working that is constantly developing. The complexity of advocacy practice and the situations of young people's lives mean that whatever form of advocacy is used, 'both the intent and outcome' of advocacy 'should increase the individual's sense of power, help them feel more confident, to become more assertive and gain increased choices' (Brandon 1995: 1). All forms of advocacy can be viewed as a means of enabling the empowerment of young service users. However, if children and young people are to come to voice, the starting point for independent advocates is to continue to make visible the paradoxical discourses that emanate from the exercise of adult power. Understanding advocacy means recognizing that barriers to the unsettlement of power relations are both subtle and overt. This means that if advocacy is to make a difference, systemic advocacy needs to be an important element of issue-based advocacy practice.

# References

Adams, R., Dominelli, L. and Payne, M. (2002) *Critical Practice in Social Work*. Basingstoke: Palgrave.

Advocacy (2000) *Principles and Standards in Independent Advocacy Organizations and Groups*. Edinburgh: Advocacy.

Advocacy in Action (1990) *A Model for User Consultation*. Nottingham: Advocacy in Action.

Aiers, A. and Kettle, J. (1998) *When Things Go Wrong: Young People's Experience of Getting Access to the Complaints Procedure in Residential Care*. London: National Institute for Social Work.

Alldred, P. (1998) Ethnography and discourse analysis: dilemmas in representing the voices of children, in J. Ribbens and R. Edwards (eds.) *Feminist Dilemmas in Qualitative Research*. London: Sage.

Archard, D. (1993) *Children, Rights and Childhood*. London: Routledge.

Arnstein, S. (1969) A ladder of citizen participation in the USA, *Journal of the American Institute of Planners*, 35 (4): 216–224.

Asist (2006) Non-Instructed Advocacy: *The Watching Brief: A policy for offering advocacy to people who do not have a system of communication that is recognised by the advocate*. Staffordshire: Assist Advocacy Services.

Atkinson, D. (1999) *Advocacy: A Review*. Brighton: Pavilion Publishing Ltd./Joseph Rowntree Foundation.

Badham, B. (2002) Preface, in C. Willow (ed.) *Participation in Practice: Children and Young People as Partners in Change*. London: The Children's Society.

Bainham, A. (2005) *Children: The Modern Law*, 3rd edn. Bristol: Family Law/Jordon Publishing.

Baldwin, M.A. (1993) Patient advocacy: a concept analysis, *Nursing Standard*, 7 (21): 33–39.

Ball, M. (2003) *School Inclusion: The School, the Family and the Community*. York: Joseph Rowntree Foundation.

Banks, S. (2001) *Ethics and Values in Social Work*, 2nd edn. Basingstoke: Palgrave.

Barber, T. and Naulty, M. (2005). Your place or mine: A research study exploring young people's participation in community planning. Dundee: University of Dundee, Youth Link Publications (retrieved from: http://www.youthlink.co.uk/docs/Practice%20Development/Your%20Place%20or%20Mine%20report.pdf).

Barclay Report (1982) *Social Workers: Their Role and Tasks*. London: Bedford Square Press.

Barford, R. and Wattam, C. (1991) Children's participation in decision making, *Practice*, 5 (2): 93–101.

Barnes, M. and Shardlow, P. (1997) From passive recipient to active citizen: participation in mental health user groups, *Journal of Mental Health*, 6 (3): 289–300.

BASW (2002) *The Code of Ethics for Social Work*. Birmingham: British Association of Social Workers.

Bateman, N. (1995) *Advocacy Skills: A Handbook for Human Service Professionals*. Aldershot: Arena.

Bateman, N. (2000) *Advocacy Skills for Health and Social Care Practitioners*, 2nd edn. London: Jessica Kingsley.

Bell, M. (2002) Promoting children's rights through the use of relationship, *Child and Family Social Work*, 7 (13): 1–11.

Bennett, O. (1999) Advocacy in nursing, *Nursing Standard*, 14 (11): 40–41.

Beresford, P. (2005) Service-user involvement in evaluation and research: issues, dilemmas and destinations, in D. Taylor and S. Balloch (eds.) *The Politics of Evaluation: Participation and Policy Implementation*. Bristol: The Policy Press.

Beresford, P. and Croft, S. (2000) Service users' knowledges and social work theory: conflict or collaboration?, *British Journal of Social Work*, 30: 489–503.

Boylan, J. (2005). Reviewing your review: A critical analysis of the role and impact of advocacy in statutory reviews of children and young people looked after by their local authority. Unpublished PhD thesis, University of Staffordshire.

Boylan, J. (2008) An analysis of the role of advocacy in promoting looked after children's participation in statutory reviews, in C. Oliver and J. Dalrymple (eds.) *Developing Advocacy for Children and Young People: Current Issues in Research and Practice*. London: Jessica Kingsley.

Boylan, J. and Boylan, P. (1998) Promoting young people's empowerment: advocacy in North Wales, *Representing Children*, 11 (1): 42–48.

Boylan, J. and Braye, S. (2006) Paid, professionalised and proceduralised: can legal and policy frameworks for child advocacy give voice to children and young people?, *Journal of Social Welfare and Family Law*, 28 (3/4): 233–249.

Boylan, J. and Dalrymple, J. (2006) Contemporary advocacy: practice for children and young people, *Childright*, 223: 28–30.

Boylan, J. and Ing, P. (2005) 'Seen and not heard': young people's experience of advocacy, *International Journal of Social Welfare*, 14: 2–12.

Boylan, J. and Wylie, J. (1999) Advocacy and child protection, in N. Parton and C. Wattam (eds.) *Child Sexual Abuse: Responding to the Experiences of Children*. Chichester: Wiley.

Brammer, A. (2007) *Social Work Law*, 2nd edn. Harlow: Longman.

Brandon, D. (1995) *Advocacy: Power to People with Disabilities*. Birmingham: Venture Press.

Braye, S. (2000) Participation and involvement in social care: an overview, in H. Kemshall and R. Littlechild (eds.) *User Involvement and Participation in Social Care*. London: Jessica Kingsley.

Bray, S. and Preston-Shoot, M. (1995) *Empowering Practice in Social Care.* Buckingham: Open University Press.

Bridge, G. (1999) Putting the Children Act Independent Person Procedure under the spotlight, *Social Policy and Administration*, 33 (2): 197–213.

Buchanan, A. and Walmsley, J. (2006) Self-advocacy in historical perspective, *British Journal of Learning Disabilities*, 34 (3): 133–138.

Bull, D. (1989) The social worker's advocacy role: a British quest for a Canadian perspective, *Canadian Social Work Review*, 6 (1): 49–68.

Burke, B. and Harrison, P. (1998) Anti-oppressive practice, in R. Adams, L. Dominelli, and M. Payne (eds.) *Social Work: Themes, Issues and Critical Debates.* Basingstoke: Macmillan.

Butler, G. and Rumsey, H. (2000) *Hearing Children's Voices: Myth or Reality.* Chichester: University College

Butler-Sloss, L.J.E. (1988) *Report of the Inquiry into Child Abuse in Cleveland* (The Cleveland Report). London: HMSO.

Cairns, L. (2006) Participation with a purpose, in K. Tisdall, J. Davis, M. Hill, and A. Prout (eds.) *Children, Young People and Social Inclusion: Participation for What?* Bristol: Policy Press.

CAIT (2002) Comments on the National Standards for Agencies providing advocacy for children and young people. Citizen Advocacy Information and Training. Accessed on-line www.citizensinformationboard.ie/publications/social/downloads/submission_Draft_Quality_Standards_Residential_Services_oct08.doc

CCETSW (1995) *Rules and Requirements for the Diploma in Social Work.* CCETSW Paper #30, revised edn. London: Central Council for Education and Training in Social Work.

Chambon, A.S. (1999) Foucault's approach: making the familiar visible, in A.S. Chambon, A. Irving, and L. Epstein (eds.) *Reading Foucault for Social Work.* New York: Colombia University Press.

Chase, E., with Simon, A., Wigfall, V., Warwick, I. and Heathcote, S. (2006) *Findings from an Evaluation of the Voice Advocacy Service.* London: Thomas Coram Research Unit.

Children and Young People Committee (2008) *Advocacy Services for Children and Young People in Wales.* Cardiff: National Assembly for Wales.

Children's Advocacy Consortium, Memorandum submitted to the House of Commons Children, Schools and Families Committee (2008) Children and Young Person's Bill [Lords]. First Report of Session 2007–2008. *Report, together with formal minutes, oral and written evidence.* HC 359. London: The Stationery Office Ltd.

Children's Commissioner for Wales (2005) *Children don't Complain.* The Children's Commissioner for Wales' review of the operation of complaints and representations and whistleblowing procedures, and arrangements for the provision of children's advocacy services in local education authorities in Wales. Swansea: Children's Commissioner for Wales.

Children's Rights Alliance for England (2003) *The Case for a Children's Rights Commisisoner for England's 11.3 Million Children*. London: CRAE.

Clark, A. and Percy-Smith, B. (2006) Beyond consultation: participatory practices in everyday spaces, *Children, Youth and Environments*, 16 (2): 1–9.

Clarke, P. (2003) *Telling Concerns*. Report of the Children's Commissioner for Wales' review of the operation of complaints and representations and whistleblowing procedures, and arrangements for the provision of children's advocacy services. Swansea: Children's Commissioner for Wales.

Clifford, D. (1998) *Social Assessment Theory and Practice*. Aldershot: Ashgate Publishing.

Clifford, D. and Burke, B. (2001) What *practical* difference does it make? Anti-oppressive ethics and informed consent, *Practice*, 3 (3): 17–29.

Clifton, C. and Hodgson, D. (1997) Rethinking practice through a children's rights perspective, in C. Cannan and C. Warren (eds.) *Social Action with Children and Families: A Community Development Approach to Children and Family Welfare*. London: Routledge.

Cloke, C. and Davies, M. (1995) Participation and empowerment in child protection, in C. Cloke and M. Davies (eds.) *Participation and Empowerment in Child Protection*. Chichester: Wiley.

Code, L. (2000) The perversion of autonomy and the subjection of women: discourses of social advocacy at century's end, in C. Mackenzie and N. Stoljar (eds.) *Relational Autonomy: Feminist Perspectives on Autonomy Agency and the Social Self*. Oxford: Oxford University Press.

Coles, B. (1995) *Youth and Social Policy: Youth Citizenship and Young Careers*. London: UCL Press

Cooke, B. and Kothari, U. (2001) The case for participation as tyranny, in B. Cooke and U. Kothari (eds.) *Participation: The New Tyranny*. New York: Zed Books.

Cousins, W., Milner, S. and McLaughlin, E. (2003) Listening to children, speaking for children: health and social services complaints and child advocacy, *Child Care in Practice*, 9 (2): 109–116.

CRAE (2003) *The Case for a Children's Rights Commissioner for England's 11.3 Million Children*. London, Children's Rights Alliance for England.

Creegan, C., Henderson, G., and King, G. (2006) *Getting it Right for Every Child: Big Words and Big Tables*. Edinburgh: Scottish Executive.

Crick, B. (1998) *Education for Citizenship and the Teaching of Democracy in Schools*. London: Quality and Curriculum Authority.

CROA (2000) *Total Respect*. London: CROA.

Croft, S. and Beresford, P. (1995) Whose empowerment? Equalising the competing discourses in community care, in R. Jack (ed.) *Empowerment in Community Care*. London: Chapman & Hall.

Crowley, A. (2006) *Scoping Paper on Pupil Participation*. Unpublished document for the Welsh Assembly Government.

Crowley, A. and Pithouse, A. (2008) Advocacy in complaints procedures: the perspectives of young people, in C. Oliver and J. Dalrymple (eds.) *Developing Advocacy for Children and Young People*. London: Jessica Kingsley.

Cutler, D. (2002) *Taking the Initiative: Promoting Young People's Involvement in Public Decision Making in the UK*. London: Carnegie Young People's Initiative.

Dalrymple, J. (1993) Advice, advocacy and representation for children, *ChildRight*, 9: 11–13.

Dalrymple, J. (1995) It's not as easy as you think! Dilemmas and advocacy, in J. Dalrymple and J. Hough (eds.) *Having a Voice: An Exploration of Children's Rights and Advocacy*. Birmingham: Venture Press.

Dalrymple, J. (2001) Safeguarding young people through confidential advocacy services, *Child and Family Social Work*, 6 (2): 149–160.

Dalrymple, J. (2003) Professional advocacy as a force for resistance in child welfare, *British Journal of Social Work*, 33: 1043–1062.

Dalrymple, J. (2004a) Constructions of child and youth advocacy: emerging issues in advocacy practice, *Children and Society*, 19: 3–15.

Dalrymple, J. (2004b) Developing the concept of professional advocacy: an examination of the role of child and youth advocates in England and Wales, *Journal of Social Work*, 4 (2): 179–197.

Dalrymple, J. (2005) *Child Protection Conferences in Wiltshire*. Bristol, University of the West of England.

Dalrymple, J. (2007) Children and young people's participation in family group conferences, in C. Ashley and P. Nixon (eds.) *Family Group Conferences – Where Next?* London: Family Rights Group.

Dalrymple, J. (2008) *Mapping the Maze: An Evaluation of the Maze Advocacy Project*. Bristol: University of the West of England.

Dalrymple, J. and Burke, B. (1995) *Anti-oppressive Practice: Social Care and the Law*. Buckingham: Open University Press.

Dalrymple, J. and Burke, B. (2000) Anti-oppressive practice, in M. Davies (ed.) *The Blackwell Encyclopaedia of Social Work*. Oxford: Blackwell.

Dalrymple, J. and Burke, B. (2006) *Anti-oppressive Practice: Social Care and the Law*, 2nd edn. Maidenhead: Open University Press.

Dalrymple, J. and Horan, H. (2008a) Advocacy in child protection conferences, in C. Oliver and J. Dalrymple (eds.) *Developing Advocacy for Children and Young People: Current Issues in Research, Policy and Practice*. London: Jessica Kingsley.

Dalrymple, J. and Horan, H. (2008b) Best practice in child advocacy: Matty's story, in K. Jones, B, Cooper, and H. Ferguson (eds.) *Best Practice in Social Work: Critical Perspectives*. Basingstoke: Palgrave Macmillan.

Dalrymple, J. and Hough, J. (eds.) (1995) *Having a Voice: An Exploration of Children's Rights and Advocacy*. Birmingham: Venture Press.

Dalrymple, J. and Oliver, C. (2008) Advocacy, participation and voice, in

J. Dalrymple and C. Oliver (eds.) *Developing Advocacy for Children and Young People: Current Issue in Research, Policy and Practice*. London: Jessica Kingsley.

Dalrymple, J. and Payne, M. (1995) *They Listened to Him*. A Report to the Calouste Gulbenkian Foundation. Manchester: ASC and the Department of Applied Community Studies, Manchester Metropolitan University.

Daniel, P. and Ivatts, J. (1998) *Children and Social Policy*. Basingstoke: Macmillan.

Dearden, C. and Becker, S. (2000) Listening to children: meeting the needs of young carers, in H. Kemshall and R. Littlechild (eds.) *User Involvement and Participation in Social Care: Research Informing Practice*. London: Jessica Kingsley.

Denney, D. (1998) *Social Policy and Social Work*. Oxford: Oxford University Press.

Department for Education and Employment (1999) *Social Inclusion: Pupil Support*, Circular 10/99. London: DfEE Publications.

Department for Education and Skills (2001a) *Special Educational Needs Code of Practice*. Nottingham: DfES Publications.

Department for Education and Skills (2001b) *Special Educational Needs Toolkit. Section 10: Transitions Planning*. Nottingham: DfES Publications.

Department for Education and Skills (2003) *Every Child Matters*. London: DfES Publications.

Department for Education and Skills (2004) *National Service Framework for Children, Young People and Maternity Services*. London: DoH/DfES Publications.

Department for Education and Skills (2005) *Guidance on the Children and Young People's Plan*. Nottingham: DfES Publications.

Department for Education and Skills (2006) *Children Looked After by Local Authorities: Year Ending 31 March 2005*. Norwich: The Stationery Office.

Department for Education and Skills (2007) *Care Matters: Time for Change*. Norwich: The Stationery Office.

Department of Health (1991) *The Right to Complain: Practice Guidance on Complaints Procedures in Social Services Departments*. London: HMSO.

Department of Health (1999) Listen up . . ., *Quality Protects Newsletter*, 2.

Department of Health (2001) *Valuing People: A New Strategy for Learning Disabilities for the 21st Century*. London: The Stationery Office.

Department of Health (2002) *National Standards for the Provision of Children's Advocacy Services*. London: DoH Publications.

Department of Health (2006a) *Transition: Getting it Right for Young People*. London: DoH.

Department of Health (2006b) *Working Together to Safeguard Children: A Guide to Inter-agency Working to Safeguard and Promote the Welfare of Children*. London: The Stationery Office.

Department of Health (2008) *Transition: Moving On*. London: DoH.

Department of Health and Children (2000) *Report of the Public Consultation for the National Children's Strategy: Our Children, Their Lives*. Dublin: Department of Health and Children.

Department of Health, Home Office and Department for Education and Employment (1999) *Working Together to Safeguard Children: A Guide to Inter-agency Working to Safeguard and Promote the Welfare of the Child*. London: The Stationery Office.

Designs for Change (1983) *Child Advocacy and the Schools: Past Impact and Potential for the 1980's*. Chicago, IL: Designs for Change.

Donnelly, J. (2003) *Universal Human Rights in Practice*. Ithaca, NY: Cornell University Press.

Downs, S.W., Costin, L.B., and McFadden, E.J. (1997) *Child Welfare and Family Services: Policies and Practice*, 5th edn. New York: Longman.

Dubois, B. and Krogsrund Miley, K. (1992) *Social Work: An Empowering Profession*. Boston, MA: Allyn & Bacon.

Eby, M. (2000) The challenge of values and ethics in practice, in A. Brechin, H. Brown, and M.A. Eby (eds.) *Critical Practice in Health and Social Care*. London: Sage.

Eustace, A. (2002). Speaking up (available at: http://www.communitycare.co.uk/Articles/2002/01/10/34601/speaking-up.html). London: Community Care.

Farnfield, S. (1997) *The Involvement of Children in Child Protection Conferences – Summary of Findings*. Reading: University of Reading.

Farrow, A. (2006) A national voice becomes independent: reflections on a journey, in *A National Voice: Self Governance and Beyond*. Leicester: National Youth Agency.

Farson, R. (1978) *Birthrights*. Harmondsworth: Penguin.

Ferguson, H. (2004) *Protecting Children in Time: Child Abuse, Child Protection and the Consequences of Modernity*. Basingstoke: Palgrave Macmillan.

Ferguson, H. (2005) Working with violence, the emotions and psychosocial dynamics of child protection: reflections on the Victoria Climbie case, *Social Work Education*, 24 (7): 781–795.

Fielding, M. (2006) Leadership, radical collegiality and the necessity of person-centred education, ESRC Teaching and Learning Research Programme (TLRP) Thematic Seminar Series, 'Contexts, communities, networks: Mobilising learners' resources and relationships in different domains'. Seminar 4: Cultures, values, identities and power, University of Exeter. Education-line, pp. 1–16. Leeds: British Education Index.

Flekkoy, M.G. (1988) Child advocacy in Norway, *Children and Society*, 4: 307–318.

Flekkoy, M.G. (1991) *A Voice for Children: Speaking Out as Their Ombudsman*. London: Jessica Kingsley.

Flekkoy, M.G. (1995) The Scandinavian experience of children's rights, in B. Franklin (ed.) *The Handbook of Children's Rights: Comparative Policy and Practice*. London: Routledge.

Flekkoy, M.G. and Kaufman, N.H. (1997) *The Participation Rights of the Child: Rights and Responsibilities in Family and Society*. London: Jessica Kingsley.

Foucault, M. (1988) *Politics, Philosophy and Culture*. London: Routledge.

Fook, J. (2002) *Social Work: Critical Theory and Practice*. London: Sage.

Fox-Harding, L.M. (1996) Recent developments in 'children's rights': liberation for whom?, *Child and Family Social Work*, 1: 141–150.

Franklin, B. (ed.) (1986) *The Rights of Children*. Oxford: Blackwell.

Franklin, B. (1995) The case for children's rights: a progress report, in B. Franklin (ed.) *Children's Rights: Comparative Policy and Practice*. London: Routledge.

Franklin, B. (ed.) (2002) *The New Handbook of Children's Rights: Comparative Policy and Practice*, 2nd edn. London: Routledge.

Freeman, M. (1983) *The Rights and Wrongs of Children*. London: Francis Pinter.

Freeman, M. (2000) The future of children's rights, *Children and Society*, 14: 277–293.

Freeman, M. (2002) Children's rights ten years after ratification, in B. Franklin (ed.) *The New Handbook of Children's Rights: Comparative Policy and Practice*. London: Routledge.

Frost, N. and Stein, M. (1999) *The Politics of Child Welfare: Inequality, Power and Change*. Hemel Hempstead: Harvester Wheatsheaf.

Foucault, M. (1988) *Politics, Philosophy and Culture*. London: Routledge.

Gates, B. (1994) *Advocacy: A Nurse's Guide*. London: Scutari Press.

Gillies, V. (2005) Meeting parents' needs? Discourses of 'support' and 'inclusion' in family policy, *Critical Social Policy*, 25 (1): 70–90.

Glaister, A. (2008) Introducing critical practice, in S. Fraser and S. Matthews (eds.) *The Critical Practitioner in Social Work and Health Care*. Milton Keynes: Open University/Sage.

Goldson, B. (2001) The demonisation of children, in P. Foley, J. Roche, and S. Tucker (eds.) *Children in Society: Contemporary Theory, Policy and Practice*. Basingstoke: Palgrave.

Goldstein, J., Freud, A., and Solnit, A. (1980) *Beyond the Best Interests of the Child*. New York: Free Press.

Goldstein, J., Solnit, A., Goldstein, S., and Freud, A. (1996). *The Best Interests of the Child: The Least Detrimental Alternative*. New York: Free Press.

Goodley, D. (2000) *Self-advocacy in the Lives of People with Learning Difficulties*. Buckingham: Open University Press.

Goodley, D. and Armstrong, D. (2001) *Self-advocacy, Civil Rights and the Social Model of Disability*. Leeds: Centre for Disability Studies/ESRC.

Graham, M. (2007a) *Black Issues in Social Work and Social Care*. Bristol: Policy Press.

Graham, M. (2007b) Giving voice to black children: an analysis of social agency, *British Journal of Social Work*, 37 (8): 1305–1317.

Harnett, R. (2003) *Peer Advocacy for Children and Young People*. Highlight No. 202. London: National Children's Bureau.

Harnett, R. (2004) Doing peer advocacy: insights from the field, *Representing Children*, 17 (2): 131–141.

Hart, R. (1992) *Children's Participation: From Tokenism to Citizenship*. Innocenti

Essays No. 4. Florence: UNICEF International Child Development Centre.

Hart, R. (1997) *Children's Participation: The Theory and Practice of Involving Young Citizens in Community Development and Environmental Care*. London: Earthscan Publications.

Harvey, J. (ed.) (1993) *The UN Convention on the Rights of the Child in Australia*. Adelaide, SA: South Australia Children's Interest Bureau.

Haynes, K. and Mickelson, J.S. (1997) *Affecting Change: Social Workers in the Political Arena*. New York: Longman.

Healy, K. (1998) Participation and child protection: the importance of context, *British Journal of Social Work*, 28: 897–914.

Henderson, R. and Pochin, M. (2001) *A Right Result? Advocacy, Justice and Empowerment*. Bristol: The Policy Press.

Hendrick, H. (2000) The child as a social actor in historical sources: problems of identification and interpretation, in P. Christensen and A. James (eds.) *Research with Children: Perspectives and Practices*. London: Falmer Press.

Hendrick, H. (2003) *Child Welfare: Historical Dimensions, Contemporary Debate*. Bristol: Policy Press.

Hendrick, H. (ed.) (2005) *Child Welfare: An Essential Reader*. Bristol: Policy Press.

Herbert, M.D. (1989) *Standing Up for Kids: Case Advocacy for Children and Youth, Strategies and Techniques*. Alberta: Office of the Children's Advocate.

Herbert, M.D. and Mould, J.W. (1992) The advocacy role in public child welfare, *Child Welfare*, 71 (2): 114–130.

Hick, S. and McNutt, J. (2002) Communities and advocacy on the internet, in S. Hick and J. McNutt (eds.) *Advocacy, Activism and the Internet: Community Organisation and Social Policy*. Chicago, IL: Lyceum Press.

Hickey, S. and Mohan, G. (2004) *Participation: From Tyranny to Transformation?* London: Zed Books.

Hill, M. and Tisdall, K. (1997) *Children and Society*. London: Longman.

Hirschman, O. (1970) *Exit, Voice and Loyalty*. Cambridge, MA: Harvard University Press.

Hodgson, D. (1995) Advocating self-advocacy – partnership to promote the rights of young people with learning disabilities, in J. Dalrymple and J. Hough (eds.) *Having a Voice: An Exploration of Children's Rights and Advocacy*. Birmingham: Venture Press.

Hoggett, P. (2000) *Emotional Life and the Politics of Welfare*. Basingstoke: Macmillan.

Holt, J. (1975) *Escape from Childhood: The Needs and Rights of Children*. Harmondsworth: Penguin.

hooks, b. (1989) *Talking Back: Talking Feminist, Thinking Black*. Boston: South End Press.

hooks, b. (1994) *Teaching to Transgress: Education as the Practice of Freedom*. London: Routledge.

House of Commons Committee (2008) The Select Committee on Children, Schools and Families Session 2007–08.

Hutt, J. (2008) *New Service Framework for the Future Provision of Advocacy Services for Children in Wales*. Written Statement by the Welsh Assembly Government. Cardiff: Welsh Assembly Government

International Association of Schools of Social Work (IASSW) and International Federation of Social Workers (IFSW) (2001) International definition of social work (available at: http://www.iassw.soton.ac.uk).

Ivers, V. (1998) Advocacy, in Y.J. Craig (ed.) *Advocacy, Counselling and Mediation in Casework*. London: Jessica Kingsley.

James, A. and Prout, A. (1990) Re-presenting childhood: time and transition in the study of childhood, in A. Prout and A. James (eds.) *Constructing and Reconstructing Childhood: Comtemporary Issues in the Sociological Study of Childhood*. Basingstoke: Falmer Press.

James, G. (1992) Theory into practice: lessons from one English organisation, in D.A. Freeman and E. Veerman (eds.) *The Ideologies of Children's Rights*. Dordrecht: Martinus Nijhoff.

Jeffs, T. (2005) Citizenship, youth work and democratic renewal, *The Encycolpaedia of Informal Education* (available at: www.infed.org/association/citizenship_youth_work_democratic_renewal).

Jenkins, P. (1995) Advocacy and the UN Convention on the Rights of the Child, in J. Dalrymple and J. Hough (eds.) *Having a Voice: An Exploration of Children's Rights and Advocacy*. Birmingham: Venture Press.

Jenkins, P. (2003) *Exploring Children's Rights: A Participative Exercise to Introduce the Issues around Children's Rights in England and Wales*. Brighton: Pavilion.

Jenks, C. (1996) *Childhood*. London: Routledge.

John, M. (1996) Voicing: research and practice with the 'silenced', in M. John (ed.) *Children in Charge: The Child's Right to a Fair Hearing*. London: Jessica Kingsley.

Johnson, T. (1989) *Professions and Power*. London: Macmillan.

Kemmis, S. (2001) Exploring the relevance of critical theory for action research: emancipatory action research in the footsteps of Jurgen Habermas, in B. Reason and H. Bradbury (eds.) *The Handbook of Action Research, Particpatory Enquiry and Practice*. London: Sage.

Kennedy, S. (1990) Politics, Poverty and Power, *Social Work Today*, 14 June, 16–17.

Kilbrandon Report (1964) *Children and Young Persons*, Cmnd 2306. London: HMSO.

Kilkelly, U. and Lundy, L. (2006) Children's rights in action: using the UN Convention on the Rights of the Child as an auditing tool, *Child and Family Law Quarterly*, 18 (3): 331–347.

Kilkelly, U., Kilpatrick, R., Lundy, L., Moore, L., Scraton, P., Davey, C. et al. (2008) *Children's Rights in Northern Ireland*. Belfast: NICCY & Queens University.

King, M. (1994) Panel games, *ChildRight*, 98: 10–12.

King, P. and Young, I. (1992) *The Child as Client*. Bristol: Family Law.

Kirby, P. (1999) *Involving Young Researchers*. York: York Publishing Services.

Kirby, P. and Bryson, S. (2002) *Measuring the Magic? Evaluating and Researching Children and Young People's Participation in Public Decision Making*. London: CYPI.

Kirby, P., Lanyon, C., Cronin, L., and Sinclair, R. (2003) *Building a Culture of Participation: Involving Children and Young People in Policy, Service Planning, Delivery and Evaluation*. London: DfES.

KLDA (2002) *Policy Guidelines: A Guide to Advocacy*. Devizes: KLDA.

Knight, A. and Oliver, C. (2007) Advocacy for disabled children and young people: benefits and dilemmas, *Child and Family Social Work*, 12 (4): 417–425.

Lansdown, G. (1995) Children's rights to participation: a critique, in C. Cloke and M. Davies (eds.) *Participation and Empowerment in Child Protection*. Chichester: Wiley.

Lansdown, G. (1997) The case for a Children's Rights Commissioner, *Children First*, Winter, pp. 17–21.

Lansdown, G. (2001) Children's welfare and children's rights, in P. Foley, J. Roche, and S. Tucker (eds.) *Children in Society: Contemporary Theory, Policy and Practice*. Basingstoke: Palgrave in association with the Open University.

Lansdown, G. (2005) *The Evolving Capacities of the Child*. Florence: Innocenti Research Centre, UNICEF.

Lavalette, M. and Cunningham, S. (2002) The sociology of childhood, in B. Goldson, M. Lavalette, and J. McKechnie (eds.) *Children, Welfare and the State*. London: Sage.

Laws, S. and Kirby, P. (2007) *Under the Table or at the Table? Supporting Children and Families in Family Group Conferences – A Summary of the Daybreak Research*. Brighton and Hove: Brighton and Hove Children's Fund Partnership and Brighton and Hove Daybreak Project.

Lawton, S. (2006) *A Voice of their Own: A toolbox of ideas and information for non-instructed advocacy*. Kidderminster: BILD Publications.

Lee, N. (2001) *Childhood and Society*. Buckingham: Open University Press.

Lee, N. (2005) *Childhood and Human Value Development: Separation and Separability*. Maidenhead: Open University Press.

Lee, S. (2007) *The Independent Mental Capacity Advocate (IMCA): Helping People who are Unable to Make Some Decisions Themselves*. London: The Mental Capacity Implementation Programme.

Levy, A. and Kahan, B. (1991) *The Pindown Experience and the Protection of Children*. The Report of the Staffordshire Child Care Enquiry 1990. Stafford: Staffordshire County Council.

Lindsay, M. (1991) Complaints procedures and their limitations in the light of the 'Pindown Inquiry', *Journal of Social Welfare Law*, 6: 432–441.

Lindsay, M. (1992) *Highlight: An Introduction to Children's Rights*. London: National Children's Bureau.

Lindsay, M. (1998). Foreword, in *On the Rights Track*. London: LGA/CROA.

Lister, R. (2008) Unpacking Children's Citizenship, in A. Inzernizzi and J. Williams *Children and Citizenship* London: Sage, pp. 9–19.

Lukes, S. (1974) *Power: A Radical View*. London: Macmillan.

Maguire, P. (2001) Uneven ground: feminisms and action research, in H. Bradbury and P. Reason (eds.) *Handbook of Action Research: Participative Inquiry and Practice*. London: Sage.

Mallick, M. (1998) Advocacy in nursing: perceptions and attitudes of the nursing elite in the United Kingdom, *Journal of Advanced Nursing*, 28 (5): 1001–1011.

Marshall, T. H. (1950) *Citizenship and Social Class and Other Essays*. Cambridge: Cambridge University Press.

McCall, G.J. (1978). The advocate social scientist: a cross-disciplinary perspective, in G.H. Weber and G.J. McCall (eds.) *Social Scientists as Advocates: Views from the Applied Professions*. Beverly Hills, CA: Sage.

Melton, G. (1987) Children, politics and morality: the ethics of child advocacy, *Journal of Clinical Child Psychology*, 16 (4): 357–367.

Mercer, K. (2009) Non-directed Advocacy, in CROA *Further Down the Rights Track*. Belper: CROA.

Mickelson, J.S. (1995) Advocacy, in R.L. Edwards (Ed.-in-Chief), *Encyclopedia of Social Work*, Vol. 1 (19th edn.). Washington, DC: NASW Press.

Minow, M. (1987) Interpreting rights: an essay for Robert Cover, *Yale Law Journal*, 96 (8): 1860–2017.

Molander, H. (1996) A child against the state: tasks of the Children's Ombudsman, in E. Verhellen (ed.) *Monitoring Children's Rights*. Amsterdam: Kluwer Law International.

Morgan, R. (2008) *Children's Views on Advocacy*. A Report by the Children's Rights Director for England. London: Ofsted.

Moss, M., Sharpe, S., and Fay, C. (1990) *Abuse in the Care System: A Pilot Study by the National Association of Young People in Care*. London: NAYPIC.

Murray, C. and Hallett, C. (2000) Young people's participation in decisions affecting their welfare, *Childhood*, 7 (1): 11–25.

National Assembly for Wales (2000) *Working Together to Safeguard Children: A Guide to Inter-agency Working to Safeguard and Promote the Welfare of Children*. Cardiff: National Assembly for Wales.

Negarandeh, R., Oskouie, F., Ahmadi, F., Nikravesh, M., and Rahm Hallberg, I. (2006) Patient advocacy: barriers and facilitators, *BMC Nursing*, 5 (3) (DOI: 10.1186/1472–6955–5–3).

Newell, P. (1991) *The UN Convention and Children's Rights in the UK*. London: National Children's Bureau.

Newell, P. (2000) *Taking Children Seriously*. London: The Gulbenkian Foundation.

Newman, T. and Blackburn, S. (2002) *Interchange 78. Transitions in the Lives of Children and Young People: Resilience Factors. Summary of Full Report*. Edinburgh: Scottish Executive Education Department.

Noffke, S. (1998) What's a nice theory like yours doing in a practice like this? And other impertinent questions about practitioner research, *Second International Practitioner Research Conference*, 9 July 1998.

Nursing and Midwifery Council (2006) *Advocacy and Autonomy*. London: NMC.

Oliver, C. (2008) Setting the scene: funding, patterns of advocacy provision and children's access to advocacy services, in C. Oliver and J. Dalrymple (eds.) *Developing Advocacy for Children and Young People: Current Issues in Research, Policy and Practice*. London: Jessica Kingsley.

Oliver, C. and Dalrymple, J. (eds.) (2008) *Developing Advocacy for Children and Young People: Developing Issues in Research, Policy and Practice*. London: Jessica Kingsley.

Oliver, C., Knight, A., and Candappa, M. (2004) *Advocacy for Looked After Children and Children in Need: A Survey*. London: Thomas Coram Foundation.

Oliver, C., Knight, A., and Candappa, M. (2006) *Advocacy for Looked After Children and Children in Need: Achievements and Challenges*. London: Thomas Coram Research Unit.

Parry, O., Pithouse, A., Anglim, C., and Batchelor, C. (2008) 'The tip of the iceberg': children's complaints and advocacy in Wales – an insider view from complaints officers, *British Journal of Social Work*, 38 (1): 5–19.

Parton, N. (1999) Reconfiguring child welfare practices: risk, advanced liberalism, and the government of freedom, in A.S. Chambon, A. Irving, and L. Epstein (eds.) *Reading Foucault for Social Work*. New York: Colombia University Press.

Parton, N. (2006) *Safeguarding Childhood: Early Intervention and Surveillance in a Late Modern Society*. Basingstoke: Palgrave Macmillan.

Patel, S. (1995) Advocacy through the eyes of a young person, in J. Dalrymple and J. Hough (eds.) *Having a Voice: An Exploration of Children's Rights and Advocacy*. Birmingham: Venture Press.

Paul, J.L. (1977) The need for advocacy, in J.L. Paul, G.R. Neufield, and J.W. Pelosi (eds.) *Child Advocacy within the System*. Syracuse, NY: Syracuse University Press.

Payne, H. and Pithouse, A. (2006) More aspiration than achievement? Children's complaints and advocacy in health services in Wales, *Health and Social Care in the Community*, 14 (6): 563–571.

Payne, M. (1995) *Social Work and Community Care*. Basingstoke: Macmillan.

Payne, M. (1996) *What is Professional Social Work?* Birmingham: Venture Press.

Payne, M. (2000a) *Anti-bureaucratic Social Work*. Birmingham: Venture Press.

Payne, M. (2000b) *Teamwork in Multiprofesssional Care*. Basingstoke: Macmillan.

Percy-Smith, B. (2006) From consultation to social learning in community participation with young people, *Children, Youth and Environments*, 16 (2): 153–179.

Percy-Smith, B. and Malone, K. (2001) Making participation relevant to the everyday lives of children and young people, *PLA Notes*, 42: 18–22.

Pierson, J. (2008) *Going Local: Working in Communities and Neighbourhoods*. London: Routledge.

Pinchbeck, I. and Hewitt, M. (1969) *Children in English Society, Vol. 2: From the Eighteenth Century to the Children Act 1948*. London: Routledge & Kegan Paul.

Pithouse, A. and Crowley, A. (2006) Adults rule? Children, advocacy and complaints to Social Services, *Children and Society*, 21: 201–213.

Pithouse, A. and Crowley, A. (2008) Complaints and children's advocacy in Wales: getting behind the rhetoric, in C. Oliver and J. Dalrymple (eds.) *Developing Advocacy for Children and Young People: Current Issues in Research, Policy and Practice*. London: Jessica Kingsley.

Pithouse, A. and Parry, O. (2005) Children's advocacy in Wales: organisational challenges for those who commission and deliver advocacy for looked after children, *Adoption and Fostering*, 29 (4): 45–56.

Pithouse, A., Crowley, A., Parry, S., Payne, H., and Dalrymple, J. (2005) *A Study of Advocacy Services for Children and Young People in Wales: A Key Messages Report*. Cardiff: Cardiff University School of Social Sciences.

Preston, J. (1997) *1997 Annual Report*. Vancouver: Office of the Child, Family and Youth Advocate.

Qualifications and Curriculum Authority (2007) A framework of personal thinking and learning skills (Homepage of QCA) (available at: www.qca.org.uk).

Qvortrup, J. (1990) A voice for children in statistical and social accounting: a plea for children's right to be heard, in A. Prout and A. James (eds.) *Constructing and Reconstructing Childhood: Contemporary Issues in the Sociological Study of Childhood*. Basingstoke: Falmer Press.

Qvortrup, J. (1994) Childhood matters: an introduction, in J. Qvortrup, M. Bardy, G. Sgritta, and H. Wintersberger (eds.) *Childhood Matters*. Aldershot: Avebury.

Ramcharan, P. (1995) Citizen advocacy and people with learning disabilities in Wales, in R. Jack (ed.) *Empowerment in Community Care*. London: Chapman & Hall.

Rasbach, J., McCarthy, J., Smolden, T., Harris, R. and Barnes, D. (2005) *Non-instructed advocacy: work in progress*. London: Action for Advocacy.

Rees, S. (1991) Achieving Power: Practice and Policy in Social Welfare. Sydney, NSW: Allen & Unwin.

Richart, D. and Bing, S. (1989) *Fairness is a Kid's Game*. Louisville, KY: Youth Advocates.

Robinson, L. (2007) *Cross-cultural Child Development for Social Workers: An Introduction*. Basingstoke: Palgrave Macmillan.

Roche, J. (1999a) Children's rights: participation and dialogue, in J. Roche and S. Tucker (eds.) *Youth in Society*. London: Sage.

Roche, J. (1999b) Children: rights, participation and citizenship, *Childhood*, 6 (4): 473–493.

Roche, J. (2002) The Children Act 1989 and children's rights: a critical reassessment, in B. Franklin (ed.) *The New Handbook of Children's Rights: Comparative Policy and Practice*. London: Routledge.

Ronstrom, A. (1989) Sweden's Children's Ombudsman: a spokesperson for children, *Child Welfare*, 58: 123–128.

Royal College of Paediatrics and Child Health Advocacy Committee (2008) *Advocating for Children*. London: RCPCH.

Sainsbury, E. (1989) Participation and paternalism, in S. Shardlow (ed.) *The Values of Change in Social Work*. London: Routledge.

Save the Children (2007) *Submission by Save the Children UK related to the United Kingdom of Great Britain and Northern Ireland for Universal Periodic Review 1st Session Children's Rights in the UK: Key Issues of Concern*. Institutional Framework for the Promotion and Protection of Children's Human Rights. London: Save the Children.

Scottish Executive (2001) *Independent Advocacy: A Guide for Commissioners*. Norwich: The Stationery Office.

Scottish Executive (2006) *Getting it Right for Every Child: Proposals for Action. Consultation with Children and Young People*. Edinburgh: Scottish Executive.

Scraton, P. (1997) Whose 'childhood'? What 'crisis'?, in P. Scraton (ed.) *'Childhood' in 'Crisis'*. London: UCL Press.

Shade, B.J. (1991) African-American patterns of cognition, in R.L. Jones (ed.) *Black Psychology*. Hampton, VA: Cobb & Henry.

Shardlow, S. (2001) Ethical aspects of social work – a common set of values and the regulation of practice: England an example, in A. Adams, P. Erath, and S. Shardlow (eds.) *Key Themes in European Social Work*. Lyme Regis: Russell House Publishing.

Sherlock, A. (2007) Listening to children in the field of education: experience in Wales, *Child and Family Law Quarterly*, 19: 161–182.

Shier, H. (2001) Pathways to participation: openings, opportunities and obligations, *Children and Society*, 15: 107–117.

Shier, H. (2006) Pathways to participation revisited, *Middle Schooling Review*, 2: 14–19.

Shier, H. (2007) Unpublished seminar presentation for SOLAR, Bristol University of the West of England.

Shier, H. (2009) Children as Public Actors: Navigating the Tensions, *Children and Society*.

Sim, A.J. and Mackay, R. (1997) Advocacy in the UK, *Practice*, 9 (2): 5.

Simons, K. (1993) *Citizen Advocacy: The Inside View*. Bristol: Norah Fry Research Centre, University of Bristol.

Simons, K. (1998) *Home, Work and Inclusion: The Social Policy Implications of Supported Living and Employment for People with Learning Disabilities*. Layerthorpe: York Publishing Services.

Smith, C. and Woodhead, K. (1999) Justice for children, in N. Parton and C. Wattam (eds.) *Child Sexual Abuse: Responding to the Experiences of Children*. Chichester: Wiley.

Smith, J. and Ing, P. (1996) *Combating Social Exclusion: Advocacy and the Needs of Service Users*. Stoke-on-Trent: Housing and Community Research Unit.

Solomon, B. (1976) *Black Empowerment: Social Work in Oppressed Communities*. New York: Colombia University Press.

Sounds Good Project and Advocacy Resource Exchange (2005) Growing up speaking out: a guide to advocacy for young learning disabled people in transition (www.advocacyresource.net).

Spinak, J.M. (2007) When did lawyers for children stop reading Goldstein, Freud and Solnit? Lessons from the twentieth century on best interests and the role of the child advocate, *Family Law Quarterly*, 41: 393.

Spivak, G.C. (1988) *In Other Worlds: Essays in Cultural Politics*. London: Routledge.

Stahl, R. (2007) 'Don't forget about me': implementing Article 12 of the UNCRC, *International Journal of Comparative Law*, 24 (3): 427–442.

Stein, M. and Ellis, S. (1983) *Gizza say: Reviews and Young People in care*. Bradford, NAYPIC.

Taylor, M. with Johnson, R. (2002) *School Councils: Their Role in Citizenship and Personal and Social Education*. Slough: National Foundation for Educational Research.

Taylor, P. and Upward, J. (1995) *Bridge Building for Effective User Involvement in Primary Care*. Birmingham: Birmingham Family Health Services Authority.

Thomas, N. (2000) *Children, Family and the State*. Basingstoke: Macmillan.

Thomas, N. (2001) Listening to children, in P. Foley, J. Roche, and S. Tucker (eds.) *Children in Society: Contemporary Theory, Policy and Practice*. Basingstoke: Palgrave Macmillan.

Timms, J.E. (1995) *Children's Representation: A Practitioner's Guide*. London: Sweet & Maxwell.

Tisdall, K. and Davies, J. (2004) Making a difference? Bringing children's and young people's views into policy making, *Children and Society*, 18 (2): 131–142.

TOPSS UK Partnership (2003) The National Occupational Standard for Social Work. Leeds: TOPSS England.

Traustadottir, R. (2006) Learning about self-advocacy from life-history: a case study form the United States, *British Journal of Learning Disabilities*, 34 (3): 175–180.

Treseder, P. and Crowley, A. (2001) *Taking the Initiative: Promoting Young People's Participation in Decision Making in Wales*. London: Carnegie Young People's Initiative.

Trevithick, P. (2000) *Social Work Skills: A Practice Handbook*. Buckingham: Open University Press.

Tunnard, J. (1997) Mechanisms for empowerment: family group conferences and local family advocacy schemes, in C. Cannan and C. Warren (eds.) *Social Action with Children and Families: A Community Development Approach to Child and Family Welfare*. London: Routledge.

UK Children's Commissioners (2008) *UK Children's Commissioners' Report to the UN Committeee on the Rights of the Child*. London: 11 Million.

UKCC (1984) *Exercising Accountability: A Framework to Assist Nurses, Midwives and Health Visitors to Consider Ethical Aspects of Professional Practice.* London: United Kingdom Central Council for Nursing, Midwifery and Health Visiting.

UKCC (1988) *UKCC's Proposed Rules for the Standard, Kind and Content of Future Pre-registration Nursing Education* (Consultation Paper). London: United Kingdom Central Council for Nursing, Midwifery and Health Visiting.

UKCC (1998) *Guidelines for Mental Health and Learning Disabilities Nursing.* London: United Kingdom Central Council for Nursing, Midwifery and Health Visiting.

Underdown, C. (2002) I'm growing up too fast': messages from young carers, *Children and Society*, 16: 57–60.

Utting, W. (1991) *Children in Public Care.* London: The Stationery Office.

Utting, W. (1997) *People Like Us: The Report of the Review of the Safeguards for Children Living Away from Home.* London: The Stationery Office.

Voice for the Child in Care (2002) *Annual Review 2001–2002.* Cardiff: VCC.

Wagner, G. (1998) *Residential Care: A Positive Choice.* Report of the Independent Review of Residential Care. London: HMSO.

Wallis, L. and Frost, N. (1998) *Cause for Complaint: The Complaints Procedure for Young People in Care.* London: The Children's Society.

Ward, S. (1995) Users of and advocates in formal complaints procedures, in J. Dalrymple and M. Payne (eds.) *They Listened to Him: A Report to the Calouste Gulbenkian Foundation.* Manchester: ASC and Department of Applied Community Studies.

Waterhouse, R. (2003) *Lessons from 'Lost in Care': Setting the Standards.* Cardiff: Tros Gynnal.

Waterhouse, R., Clough, M., and le Fleming, M. (2000) *Lost in Care: Report of the Tribunal of Inquiry into the Abuse of Children in Care in the Former County Council Areas of Gwynedd and Clwyd since 1974*, HC 21. London: HMSO.

Wattam, C. (1999) Confidentiality and the social organisation of telling, in N. Parton and C. Wattam (eds.) *Child Sexual Abuse: Responding to the Experiences of Children.* Chichester: Wiley.

Wattam, C. and Parton, N. (1999) Impediments to implementing a child centred approach, in N. Parton and C. Wattam (eds.) *Child Sexual Abuse: Responding to the Experiences of Children.* Chichester: Wiley.

Weafer, J. (2003) *The Jigsaw of Advocacy: Finding a Voice.* Dublin: Comhairle.

Welsh Assembly Government (2003) *National Standards for the Provision of Children's Advocacy Services.* Cardiff: Welsh Assembly Government.

Welsh Assembly Government (2007) *Consultation on a New Service Model for Delivering Advocacy Services for Children and Young People.* Cardiff: Welsh Assembly Government.

Wertheimer, A. (1996) *Advocacy: The Rantzen Report.* London: BBS Educational Developments.

Wheeler, P. (2000) Is advocacy at the heart of professional practice?, *Nursing Standard*, 14 (36): 39–41.

Wildemeersch, D., Jansen, T., Vandenerbeele, J., and Jans, M. (1988) Social learning: a new perspective on learning in participatory Systems, *Studies in Continuing Education*, 20 (2): 251–265.

Williams, P. and Schoultz, B. (1982) *We Can Speak for Ourselves*. Boston, MA: Brookline Books.

Willow, C. (1998) Listening to children in local government, in D. Utting (ed.) *Children's Services: Now and in the Future*. London: National Children's Bureau Enterprises.

Willow, C. (2002) *Participation in Practice: Children and Young People as Partners in Change*. London: The Children's Society.

Willow, C. and Barry, T. (1998) *On the Rights Track: Guidance for Local Authorities on Developing Children's Rights and Advocacy Services*. London: Local Government Association/CROA.

Willow, C. and Neale, B. (2004) *Citizenship: Ideas into Practice*. York: Joseph Rowntree Foundation.

Wilson, A. and Beresford, P. (2000) 'Anti-oppressive practice': emancipation or appropriation, *British Journal of Social Work*, 30: 553–573.

Wiltshire Advocacy Project (1996) Celebration of Advocacy Conference Report, in G. Anderson (ed.) *Celebration of Advocacy*. Salisbury: Wiltshire Advocacy Project.

Wyllie, J. (1999) *The Last Rung of the Ladder: An Examination of the Use of Advocacy by Children and Young People in Advancing Participation Practice within the Child Protection System*. London: The Children's Society.

Wyllie, J. (2000) *UCAN Project Annual Report 1999/2000*. London: The Children's Society.

# Index

# WORKING WITH CHILDREN IN CARE
## EUROPEAN PERSPECTIVES

### Pat Petrie, Janet Boddy, Valerie Wigfall and Claire Cameron

- How does residential care in England compare with that of other European countries?
- What is social pedagogy, and how does it help those working with children in care?
- How can child care policy and practice be improved throughout the United Kingdom?

This book is written against the background of the gross social disadvantage suffered by most looked-after children in England. It compares European policy and approaches – from Belgium, Denmark, France, Germany and the Netherlands – to the public care system in England. Drawing on research from all six countries, the authors analyze how different policies and practice can affect young people in residential homes. A particular focus is on the unique approach offered by social pedagogy, a concept that is commonly used in continental Europe.

The book compares young people's own experiences and appraisals of living in a residential home, and the extent to which residential care compounds social exclusion. Based upon theoretical and empirical evidence, it offers solutions for current dilemmas concerning looked-after children in the United Kingdom, in terms of lessons learned from policy and practice elsewhere, including training and staffing issues.

*Working with Children in Care* is key reading for students, academics and professionals in health, education and social care who work with children in residential care.

### Contents
*Introduction – What is pedagogy? – National differences in policy and training for work with looked after children – Working in residential care – Understandings and values: Staff responses to hypothetical situations – Looked-after lives – Giving children a good start? – Policy and practice in England: What is it in our current situation that makes it difficult to do well? – Concluding discussion, lessons learned – Appendix*

2006    208pp
ISBN-13: 978 0 335 21634 5 (ISBN-10: 0 335 21634 X) Paperback
ISBN-13: 978 0 335 21635 2 (ISBN-10: 0 335 21635 8) Hardback

*The* **McGraw·Hill** *Companies*

# What's new from Open University Press?

Education... Media, Film & Cultural Studies

Health, Nursing & Social Welfare... Higher Education

Psychology, Counselling & Psychotherapy... Study Skills

Keep up with what's buzzing
at Open University Press
by signing up to receive
regular title information at
www.openup.co.uk/elert

Sociology

# OPEN UNIVERSITY PRESS

McGraw - Hill Education